Developing and Presenting a Professional Portfolio in Early Childhood Education

THIRD EDITION

Nancy W. Wiltz

Janese Daniels

Heather Skelley

Hannah S. Cawley

Ocie Watson-Thompson

All of Towson University

PEARSON

Boston   Columbus   Indianapolis   New York   San Francisco   Upper Saddle River
Amsterdam   Cape Town   Dubai   London   Madrid   Milan   Munich   Paris   Montreal   Toronto
Delhi   Mexico City   São Paulo   Sydney   Hong Kong   Seoul   Singapore   Taipei   Tokyo

Vice President and Editorial Director:
Jeffery W. Johnston
Senior Acquisitions Editor: Julie Peters
Editorial Assistant: Andrea Hall
Vice President, Director of Marketing:
Margaret Waples
Senior Marketing Manager: Chris Barry
Senior Managing Editor: Pamela D. Bennett
Senior Project Manager: Mary M. Irvin
Production Manager: Laura Messerly

Senior Art Director: Jayne Conte
Cover Designer: Bruce Kenselaar
Cover Art: Fotolia
Full-Service Project Management:
Nitin Agarwal/Aptara®, Inc.
Electronic Composition: Aptara®, Inc.
Printer/Binder: Edwards Brothers Malloy
Cover Printer: Edwards Brothers Malloy
Text Font: Minion Pro

Credits and acknowledgments for materials borrowed from other sources and reproduced, with permission, in this textbook appear on the appropriate page within the text.

Every effort has been made to provide accurate and current Internet information in this book. However, the Internet and information posted on it are constantly changing, so it is inevitable that some of the Internet addresses listed in this textbook will change.

Library of Congress Cataloging-in-Publication Data

Developing and presenting a professional portfolio in early childhood education / Nancy W. Wiltz . . . [et al.].—3rd ed.
  p. cm.
ISBN-13: 978-0-13-293038-3
ISBN-10: 0-13-293038-2
1. Portfolios in education.   2. Early childhood teachers—Rating of.   I. Wiltz, Nancy W.
LB1029.P67D48 2013
370.711—dc23

2012022303

10 9 8 7 6 5 4 3 2 1

ISBN 13: 978-0-13-293038-3
ISBN 10:   0-13-293038-2

Preface

Developing and Presenting a Professional Portfolio in Early Childhood Education, Third Edition, has been developed to assist preservice teachers in early childhood education in developing professional portfolios. It may be used in any of a variety of courses or entry points in your program. The book uses a step-by-step approach and numerous examples to assist early childhood education students in successfully developing a paper and/or an electronic professional teaching portfolio. Each chapter is designed to support the development of the professional portfolio in the same way we support our Towson University interns through this process.

■ New to This Edition

- The newly revised NAEYC Standards for Early Childhood Professional Preparation Programs (2009).
- The Revised InTASC Model Core Teaching Standards updated in April 2011.
- An updated review of the literature.
- The use of NAEYC Standards as the primary standards, which means that this book can be used to engage prospective early childhood professionals at community colleges as well as four-year universities.
- Activities, suggested websites, and references at the end of each chapter.
- Chapter 3, the electronic portfolio chapter, includes the Web address where readers can find the NETS standards.
- Examples of authentic prospective teacher interview questions from a Head Start center, preschool, and elementary school.

Chapter Contents

Chapter 1 explains the rationale for using a professional portfolio in early childhood education, identifies the parts of the portfolio, and describes the phases of the portfolio process. Chapter 2 explains the standards used by early childhood educators for structuring a portfolio; these standards illustrate competencies of beginning teachers in our field. Chapter 3 defines and describes electronic portfolios, discusses the benefits and challenges associated with using e-portfolios, and provides the skills needed to execute a successful e-portfolio. Chapter 4 provides guidelines for setting up a portfolio. Chapter 5 supports the writing of a strong philosophy of education statement. Chapter 6 explains what artifacts are and how they are used in portfolios to illustrate knowledge in the field. The chapter provides ideas for finding and choosing appropriate artifacts that support learning. Chapter 7 addresses the important task of writing effective reflective narratives. Chapter 8 provides suggestions for collecting, cataloging, and storing evidence for use in a showcase or interview portfolio. The goal of Chapter 9 is to help candidates organize a final showcase portfolio and prepare them for their summative assessment, the portfolio presentation. Chapter 10, the final chapter, looks at how a portfolio can prepare candidates to enter the workforce as professionals and how a portfolio may remain a valuable tool throughout a teacher's professional career.

Acknowledgments

The authors wish to acknowledge the support of the students and faculty members in the Department of Early Childhood Education and the College of Education at Towson University. All the artifacts included in *Developing and Presenting a Professional Portfolio in Early Childhood Education*, Third Edition, come from our students, who have generously allowed us to use their work. In particular, we would like to thank: Monica Borja, Janina Brugada, Elizabeth Eagling, Kathy Landis-Mullins, Lauren Lijweski, Jenn Maikin, Jennifer Palmer, Nicole Pulchino, James Rock, Miguel Rodriguez, Katie Runyon, Sarah Rybka, Jennifer Sharp, and Alexandria (Lexie) Weir.

We would also like to thank the editors and staff at Pearson, specifically Julie Peters, Andrea Hall, and Mary Irvin, whose assistance was invaluable.

About the Authors

Nancy W. Wiltz, Ph.D.

Nancy W. Wiltz earned a B.S. in Education at the University of Missouri-Columbia, and an M.A. and a Ph.D. in Curriculum and Instruction at the University of Maryland, College Park. In 1999, she joined the Early Childhood Education faculty at Towson University, where she taught pre-primary and primary curriculum courses until she left the main campus to administer a new Montgomery College–Towson University–Montgomery County Public Schools partnership in Early Childhood Education at the Universities at Shady Grove. At that location for the past three years, she taught seminar, supervised student teachers, and helped students develop their final showcase and interview portfolios. Now retired, she is a Professor Emerita from Towson University. She keeps busy writing, gardening, playing with her five grandchildren, and working as a volunteer for three former students who now teach first grade in a Montgomery County public school.

Janese Daniels, Ph.D.

Janese Daniels received her B.S. in Psychology from Morgan State University; her M.A. in Education, Instructional Systems Development, from UMBC; and her Ph.D. in Education, Human Development, from the University of Maryland, College Park. Her teaching career began in 1992 as a teacher in the Baltimore public schools. After completing her doctorate, she joined the faculty in the Department of Early Childhood Education at Towson University in 2006, where she teaches undergraduate and graduate courses in early intervention, diversity, literacy, technology, and pre-primary and primary curriculum. She has worked with Head Start and public school teachers around the country. In 2011, she piloted an e-portfolio section of early childhood education students at Towson University. She enjoys watching teacher candidates learn and grow into professionals.

Heather Skelley, M.S.

Heather Skelley received her B.S. and M.S. from Towson University, and is currently a full-time lecturer in the Department of Early Childhood Education, where she teaches reading, literacy, and curriculum courses. She is a former prekindergarten, first-grade, and second-grade classroom teacher in the Baltimore County public schools. She spent two years as a professional developer with the Fund for Educational Excellence, and currently is a professional developer for Children's Literacy Initiative, a nonprofit organization that provides literacy staff development for teachers in urban school districts. She has not only modified and written curriculum in reading for the state of Maryland, she has also, along with Hannah Cawley, co-authored several online courses. She is the busy mother of two active boys, and she is president of their school's PTA in Harford County, Maryland.

Hannah Smith Cawley, M.S.

Hannah Smith Cawley joined the department of early childhood education at Towson University as a full-time lecturer in 2003. She teaches a variety of courses in early childhood education, ranging from the introductory course to the student teaching seminar. Mrs. Cawley hails from Maine, where she completed her B.S.; her M.S. is from the University of Illinois, Champaign-Urbana. This range of experiences allows her to bring a fresh and critical eye to the portfolio-development process. With Heather Skelley, she has developed several online courses including Human Growth and Development and Introduction to Early Childhood Education. She is also a university liaison to a cluster of professional development schools in Baltimore County.

Ocie Watson-Thompson, Ed.D.

Dr. Ocie Watson-Thompson, a native of Alabama, began her career as an elementary school teacher but has taught for nearly 30 years in teacher education at Towson University. Her specialty is curriculum and instruction with concentrations in special education, literacy, and diversity. As the "guru" of portfolio at Towson University, she taught a portfolio course for many years, although now portfolio development is incorporated into all courses. As a faculty member, her course load ranged from teaching introduction to early childhood education to the final capstone student teaching seminar, helping her to clearly articulate the progressive work that goes into portfolio development and presentation. Dr. Watson-Thompson is an associate professor at Towson University, where she is currently chair of the Department of Early Childhood Education.

Contents

Appendixes

chapter 1

An Introduction to Your Portfolio

The use of a professional teaching portfolio comes from the fields of art, writing, and architecture, where professionals in those fields collect and display samples of work to showcase their talents and skills (Glatthorn, 1996). The idea of using portfolios to document proficiency in teaching is embedded in those traditions. With the onset of competency-based teacher education programs coupled with the accountability movement, portfolios have become a worthwhile process for documenting teaching performance, fostering professional growth, and facilitating reflective thinking (Bullock & Hawk, 2010). Portfolios— either paper or electronic—are one approach in determining the effectiveness of aspiring teachers. When used with other forms of assessment, portfolios provide a broad and complete picture of the preservice teacher. Most states have moved to standards-based programs built on "the idea that educators need to present evidence of their competence relative to standards" (Ashford & Deering, 2003, p. 22); thus, portfolios have became the "customary method for displaying teaching competence and content-area knowledge" (Rieman & Okrasinski, 2007, p. 2).

What Is a Portfolio?

Preparing you, the student, to be thoughtful and reflective is an important aspect of both teaching and learning. Your construction of teacher knowledge is emphasized through experiences that include planning, teaching, discussing, and reflecting on understanding in a variety of ways. In line with Dewey's notion of reflective inquiry (Dewey, 1933/1998), you are encouraged to acquire and apply knowledge simultaneously. In short, you learn by doing. A portfolio is one way to document what you have learned.

A portfolio is "an envelope of the mind" (Dietz, 1995)—an organized collection of artifacts, evidence, and reflections that represent progressive progress toward professional growth, continuous learning, and "achieved competence in the complex act called teaching" (Campbell, Cignetti, Melenyzer, Nettles, & Wyman, 2011, p. 3). Portfolios are "ongoing assessments that are composed of purposeful collections that examine achievement, effort, improvement, and processes, such as selecting, comparing, sharing, evaluating, and goal setting (Tierney, Carter, & Desai as cited in Johnson & Rose, 1997, p. 6). In higher education, portfolios document the totality of the college experience. As you change throughout your four years of college education, portfolios help you carefully look at your teaching performance, encourage your professional growth, and contribute to reflective thinking. A portfolio is more than a scrapbook. It is not merely a container for storing and displaying evidence of a teacher's knowledge and skills. A teaching portfolio is tangible evidence of the knowledge, skills, attitudes, and dispositions that you have acquired. Portfolios also assess skills, understandings, and processes, and they use a variety of evidence to record growth over time (Klenowski, 2002).

No set formula exists for preparing one's portfolio, and no two portfolios look alike. By selecting evidence of your individual strengths, a unique picture of you comes to life. However, all portfolios create a context for your teaching experiences. They provide formative evaluation in the form of self-improvement and achievement, and include rationales for the chosen artifacts. Portfolios allow you to assess strengths, reflect on goals, and identify areas for further growth. Summative evaluation occurs at the end of a two- or four-year process when you communicate a personal portrait of yourself and chronicle your development to a team of professors and teachers. Your presentation is tailored to using a variety of methods and multiple sources to document that specific standards have been met satisfactorily.

Not only does the portfolio serve as an instrument of your growth and development as a preservice intern and an emerging teacher, it also provides important information for the assessment of an early childhood education program. It serves to depict the knowledge, skills, attitudes, dispositions, and ultimately the presentation needed for effective teachers of young children. As an authentic form of assessment, portfolios are experiential, helping you as students to achieve mastery in discovery and problem solving. Portfolios differ from other types of assessment in the following ways (www.sitesupport.org/module1/teacherreflection.htm):

1. Portfolios allow the student to select from multiple sources of evidence gathered in authentic settings.
2. Portfolio development requires decision making on the part of the developer.
3. Portfolios assist in determining future professional goals.

What Is the Purpose of the Portfolio?

The main purpose of the portfolio is to document your growth and development as an emerging teacher. It allows you to see yourself grow, develop, and change over time. If you are a student at a community college, you will show growth over your first two years. If you are in a four-year program, your growth will be over all four years. Production of a portfolio always involves both process and a product. The process includes the systematic collection of, selection of, and reflection about evidence that documents the continuous growth in competencies identified by internal and external professional standards. As a product, a portfolio is a purposeful collection of evidence, arranged in an organized, manageable format that provides documentation of professional growth and achievement. Choosing and organizing text, images, photographs, sounds, video, and other artifacts to represent one's teaching beliefs and experiences involves a reflective process "that provides the greatest opportunities for professional understanding and self assessment" (www.sitesupport.org/module1/teacherreflection.htm, p. 1).

While the portfolio's primary purpose is to document and support the attainment of identified competencies, it has additional values. The production of a portfolio:

- Initiates a mindset of learning as a lifelong endeavor.
- Develops and supports reflective thinking.
- Engenders collaboration among all professional partners (interns, mentor-teachers, university faculty members).
- Places responsibility on you to shape your own professional destiny.
- Presents a more authentic picture of acquired knowledge, skills, attitudes, and dispositions.
- Provides multiple data sources to document growth and achievement.
- Facilitates goal setting.
- Integrates theory and practice.
- Contributes to and fosters best practice.

Parts of the Portfolio

According to Bullock and Hawk (2010), portfolios have four specific components:

- A specific purpose
- A targeted audience
- Meaningful evidence
- Reflective narratives

Your purpose as an emerging teacher is to demonstrate your knowledge, skills, attitudes, dispositions, and abilities related to teaching. Your targeted audience may be a group of external reviewers made up of professors and mentor-teachers who will review your work prior to graduation. It may also be a future employer. Evidence is the "stuff" that is in your portfolio—the lesson plans, student work, assessments, papers, images, photographs, audio and video clips, thematic units, and service projects involving parents and/or the community. Reflective narratives are addressed more fully in Chapter 7, but basically your reflection, written as a narrative, needs to extend your personal philosophy, provide a rationale for what you did and why you did it, clearly articulate why the evidence you are presenting fits into the chosen standard(s), and explain how this evidence contributed to student learning and your own growth as a teacher.

Stages or Phases of the Portfolio Process

Schools of education, students, and school systems have developed many types of portfolios. The five types described in this book are commonly found throughout the literature, although terminology may differ. While some books refer to these as "types" of portfolios, we emphasize that they are really stages or phases of development because each portfolio type emphasizes growth and change over time. Obviously, what you include in your portfolio depends on the purpose of your portfolio, your level of development and professionalism, and the audience for whom it is created.

Collection Portfolio

A collection portfolio is merely a compilation of evidence that can include any and all college-level experiences and activities related to your growth. Ideally, this type of portfolio is begun in your first early childhood courses. The emphasis is on collecting a variety of artifacts that document skills, knowledge, dispositions, and experiences that support your desire and potential to be a successful early childhood educator. Artifacts in this stage might include observations, interviews, article reflection papers, research papers, PowerPoint presentations, journals, projects, and assignments that feature work from early childhood theorists.

Developmental Portfolio

The developmental portfolio is a continuing collection of evidence that reflects developing competencies over a longer period of time. You are still collecting artifacts, but now you are past the early coursework phase and are focusing more on how you affect the learner. Instead of just turning in a research paper or a mock lesson plan, you now ask yourself, "How does this affect what I do with children?" This type of portfolio is sometimes called a working portfolio (Martin, 1999; Costantino & DeLorenzo, 2006) or a process portfolio (Antonek, McCormick, & Donato, 1997) because it reflects work in progress. A working portfolio is "a collection of teaching evidence and reflections displayed as paper or digital assets that provide ongoing documentation of a teacher candidate's growth at various benchmarks throughout the teacher education program" (Costantino & DeLorenzo, 2006, p. 169). But the developmental portfolio is not yet a polished document.

Artifacts for the developmental portfolio, in addition to those mentioned for the collection portfolio, might include classroom observations, child development studies, pieces of reflective writing, a variety of lesson plans implemented in a classroom, samples or lists of instructional materials created for teaching, thematic units, and projects involving parents and/or the community.

Showcase Portfolio

The showcase portfolio is a "polished collection of exemplary documents and reflective entries that highlight an in-service teacher's best work and accomplishments" (Costantino & DeLorenzo, 2006, p. 169). This type of portfolio demands much more emphasis on the selection of artifacts and shows strong evidence of how the artifacts meet your institution's identified standards and criteria. Take time to sort and review your existing artifacts. Do they showcase the type of teacher you are? Do they exemplify your best work? If not, you may want to strengthen your portfolio by paying in-depth attention to required criteria, clarifying links between your narrative reflection and the chosen artifact, and refining artifacts to better meet the indicators of each standard. Self-assessment and feedback from faculty, mentor-teachers, and peers may help you with this process. Choose a balanced selection of artifacts that document learning in all curricular areas and under all standards. Present a consistent, cumulative, and comprehensive profile of yourself that confirms your competencies and effectiveness, and that showcases your very best work.

Interview Portfolio

The interview portfolio is usually a subset of your best work from your showcase portfolio used to highlight your work for a very specific audience. Sometimes this smaller portfolio is known as a product portfolio (Antonek, McCormick, & Donato, 1997) because the end product identifies and supports effective, professional competencies; provides evidence specific to a particular district and/or position desired; and communicates evidence of your readiness to enter the teaching profession. At times an interview portfolio is known as a presentation portfolio because it is compiled "for the expressed purpose of giving others an effective and easy-to-read portrait of your professional competence" (Campbell et al., 2011, p. 4). An interview portfolio is selective and streamlined so that your material can be viewed easily. Reduce your number of artifacts to only those that support and document your strength and accomplishments as a teacher of a specific grade or school.

ACTIVITY 1-1

Now that you have an understanding of what a portfolio is, its purpose, why you would use it, and the various stages you will go through to develop a portfolio, answer the following questions:

- What is a portfolio?
- Why would you develop a professional portfolio?
- What is the value of portfolio development?
- How do you envision your portfolio evolving through the stages?
- What unique characteristics or skills do you have that you want to showcase?

Summary

This chapter has introduced you to the portfolio concept as a means of assisting you in developing a professional portfolio. You have learned that portfolios in teacher education are often based on one or more sets of standards that you will be asked to meet. Portfolios also become an authentic assessment process whereby you ultimately demonstrate your individuality, creativity, professionalism, organizational skills, writing ability, computer skills, leadership, and potential to succeed as a teacher. Through the descriptions of the various stages in the portfolio process, you have learned that portfolios are not distinct types, but rather are overlapping stages and phases of your development from student to teacher.

Suggested Websites

Washington State University provides this site that includes a general format, outline of a teaching portfolio, examples of teaching portfolios, and references. Go to:
www.wsu.edu/provost/teaching.htm.

Johns Hopkins University and Morgan State University provide a step-by-step description of the portfolio process,

additional readings, activities to support portfolio development, and examples and models of electronic portfolios. Go to:
www.sitesupport.org/.htm.

References

Antonek, J. L., McCormick, D. E., & Donato, R. (1997). The student teacher portfolio as autobiography: Developing a professional identity. *The Modern Language Journal, 81*, 5–27.

Ashford, A., & Deering, P. (2003). *Middle level teacher preparation: The impact of the portfolio experience on teachers' professional development.* Paper presented at the annual meeting of the American Educational Research Association, Chicago, IL.

Bullock, A. A., & Hawk, P. P. (2010). *Developing a teaching portfolio: A guide for preservice and practicing teachers* (3rd ed.). New York: Pearson.

Campbell, D. M., Cignetti, P. B., Melenyzer, B. J., Nettles, D. H., & Wyman, R. M. (2011). *How to develop a professional portfolio: A manual for teachers* (5th ed.). Boston, MA: Pearson.

Costantino, P. M., & DeLorenzo, M. N. (2006). *Developing a professional teaching portfolio: A guide for success* (2nd ed.). New York: Pearson.

Dewey, J. (1933/1998). *How we think: A restatement of the relation of reflective thinking to the educative process.* Boston: Houghton Mifflin.

Dietz, M. E. (1995). Using portfolios as a framework for professional development. *Journal of Staff Development, 16*(2), 40–43.

Glatthorn, A. A. (1996). *The teacher's portfolio: Fostering and documenting professional development.* Rockport, MA: ProActive.

Johnson, N., & Rose, L. (1997). *Portfolios: Clarifying, constructing, and enhancing.* Lancaster, PA: Technomic.

Klenowski, V. (2002). *Developing portfolios for learning and assessment: Processes and principles.* London: Routledge Falmer.

Martin, D. B. (1999). *The portfolio planner: Making professional portfolios work for you.* Upper Saddle River, NJ: Prentice Hall.

Rieman, P. L., & Okrasinski, J. (2007). *Creating your teaching portfolio* (2nd ed.). Boston: McGraw-Hill.

chapter 2

· ·

Using Teaching Standards to Organize Your Portfolio

Using professional standards as an organizational framework for your portfolio is one way to illustrate the relationship between your knowledge, skills, and abilities and the standards of your professional field. Those in early childhood, especially in institutions of higher education, often rely on the longstanding commitment of the National Association for the Education of Young Children (NAEYC) since this organization has been setting standards for degree programs for more than 25 years. Although updating standards is a continuous process, NAEYC's position statement on professional preparation focuses on early childhood methods and content, child development, family and community relationships, observation and assessment, effective approaches for connecting with children and families, meaningful curriculum, and professional development. Involvement in and the integration of inclusion and diversity are additional threads that cross all six standards (NAEYC Standards for Early Childhood Professional Preparation Programs, 2009).

In addition, institutions of higher learning that are endorsed by the National Council for Accreditation for Teacher Education (NCATE) use the InTASC Model Core Teaching Standards from the Council of Chief State School Officers (CCSSO) that were revised in 2011. They "outline what teachers should know and be able to do to ensure every K–12 student reaches the goal of being ready to enter college or the workforce in today's world" (Council of Chief State School Officers, 2011, p. 3). These standards are based on current research on best practices in teaching. By outlining the foundations and principles of today's teaching profession, they promote a new vision of teaching.

Who and What Is NAEYC?

The National Association for the Education of Young Children (NAEYC) is the largest and most influential organization of early childhood educators in the United States. It is dedicated solely to enhancing the lives of young children and their families through research, professional journals, conferences, and the development of standards and accreditation. For over 80 years, the organization has worked "to provide the best tools and information about early childhood development" (www.naeyc.org/teachers, p. 1) so that all children from birth through age eight who are in child-care centers, family day care, homes, and public and private schools will receive a high-quality, developmentally appropriate education. The organization supports children and their families, teachers, and administrators by providing standards for professional preparation, accrediting programs for young children, developing position statements, advocating for excellence in early childhood education, lobbying for federal legislation, publishing magazines and journals, holding conferences for early childhood educators, and promoting and disseminating research to influence public policy (www.naeyc.org). In 2009, NAEYC made substantial revisions to the standards by incorporating new knowledge and research while still maintaining the core values and principles of the founders of the early childhood profession. Specifically, the new standards include "state and national early childhood teacher credentialing, national accreditation of professional early childhood preparation programs, state approval of early childhood teacher education programs and articulation agreements between various levels and types of professional development programs" (NAEYC Standards for Early Childhood Professional Preparation Programs, 2009, p. 1).

What Are the NAEYC Standards for Early Childhood Professional Preparation Programs?

■ Standard 1. Promoting Child Development and Learning

Candidates prepared in early childhood degree programs are grounded in a child development knowledge base. They use their understanding of young children's characteristics and needs, and of multiple interacting influences on children's development and learning, to create environments that are healthy, respectful, supportive, and challenging for each child.

Key Elements of Standard 1

1a: Knowing and understanding young children's characteristics and needs, from birth through age 8.
1b: Knowing and understanding the multiple influences on early development and learning.
1c: Using developmental knowledge to create healthy, respectful, supportive, and challenging learning environments for young children.

■ Standard 2. Building Family and Community Relationships

Candidates prepared in early childhood degree programs understand that successful early childhood education depends on partnerships with children's families and communities. They know about, understand, and value the importance and complex characteristics of children's families and communities. They use this understanding to create respectful, reciprocal relationships that support and empower families, and to involve all families in their children's development and learning.

Key Elements of Standard 2

2a: Knowing about and understanding diverse family and community characteristics.

2b: Supporting and engaging families and communities through respectful, reciprocal relationships.

2c: Involving families and communities in young children's development and learning.

■ Standard 3: Observing, Documenting, and Assessing to Support Young Children and Families

Candidates prepared in early childhood degree programs understand that child observation, documentation, and other forms of assessment are central to the practice of all early childhood professionals. They know about and understand the goals, benefits, and uses of assessment. They know about and use systematic observations, documentation, and other effective assessment strategies in a responsible way, in partnership with families and other professionals, to positively influence the development of every child.

Key Elements of Standard 3

3a: Understanding the goals, benefits, and uses of assessment—including its use in development of appropriate goals, curriculum, and teaching strategies for young children.

3b: Knowing about and using observation, documentation, and other appropriate assessment tools and approaches, including the use of technology in documentation, assessment, and data collection.

3c: Understanding and practicing responsible assessment to promote positive outcomes for each child, including the use of assistive technology for children with disabilities.

3d: Knowing about assessment partnerships with families and with professional colleagues to build effective learning environments.

■ Standard 4. Using Developmentally Effective Approaches to Connect with Children and Families

Candidates prepared in early childhood degree programs understand that teaching and learning with young children is a complex enterprise, and its details vary depending on children's ages, characteristics, and the settings within which teaching and learning occur. They understand and use positive relationships and supportive interactions as the foundation for their work with young children and families. Candidates know, understand, and use a wide array of developmentally appropriate approaches, instructional strategies, and tools to connect with children and families and positively influence each child's development and learning.

Key Elements of Standard 4

4a: Understanding positive relationships and supportive interactions as the foundation of candidates' work with young children.

4b: Knowing and understanding effective strategies and tools for early education, including appropriate uses of technology.

4c: Using a broad repertoire of developmentally appropriate teaching and learning approaches.

4d: Reflecting on one's own practice to promote positive outcomes for each child.

■ Standard 5. Using Content Knowledge to Build Meaningful Curriculum

Candidates prepared in early childhood degree programs use their knowledge of academic disciplines to design, implement, and evaluate experiences that promote positive development and learning for each and every young child. Candidates understand the importance of developmental domains and academic (or content) disciplines in early childhood curriculum. They know the essential concepts, inquiry tools, and structure of content areas, including academic subjects, and can identify resources to deepen their understanding. Candidates use their own knowledge and other resources to design, implement, and evaluate meaningful, challenging curriculum that promotes comprehensive developmental and learning outcomes for every young child.

Key Elements of Standard 5

5a: Understanding content knowledge and resources in academic disciplines: language and literacy; the arts—music, creative movement, dance, drama, visual arts; mathematics; science; physical activity, physical education, and health and safety; and social studies.

5b: Knowing and using the central concepts, inquiry tools, and structures of content areas or academic disciplines.

5c: Using one's knowledge, appropriate early learning standards, and other resources to design, implement, and evaluate developmentally meaningful and challenging curriculum for each child.

■ Standard 6. Becoming a Professional

Candidates prepared in early childhood degree programs identify and conduct themselves as members of the early childhood profession. They know and use ethical guidelines and other professional standards related to early childhood practice. They are continuous, collaborative learners who demonstrate knowledgeable, reflective, and critical perspectives on their work, making informed decisions that integrate knowledge from a variety of sources. They are informed advocates for sound educational practices and policies.

Key Elements of Standard 6

6a: Identifying and involving oneself with the early childhood field.

6b: Knowing about and upholding ethical standards and other early childhood professional guidelines.

6c: Engaging in continuous, collaborative learning to inform practice; using technology effectively with young children, with peers, and as a professional resource.

6d: Integrating knowledgeable, reflective, and critical perspectives on early education.

6e: Engaging in informed advocacy for young children and the early childhood profession.

Field Experiences

"A key component of each of NAEYC's standards is hands-on field or clinical experiences . . . emphasized in [the six] NAEYC Standards" (NAEYC Standards for Early Childhood Professional Preparation Programs, 2009, p. 6). We all know that teaching can be best learned by practicing in real classrooms with supervision from experienced professors and mentors, and individual early childhood education programs must include a variety of field experiences for accreditation purposes. The professional development school movement creates a new form of education that promotes interactive partnerships with high-quality schools; integrates theory, research, and practice; and allows interns to develop and refine their skills and reflect on the social cultural, ethnic, linguistic, and economic realities of the 21st century.

What Are the InTASC Model Core Teaching Standards?

Understanding the process of developing a professional portfolio for early childhood education requires an in-depth understanding of the 10 InTASC Model Core Teaching Standards, the thoughts behind their development, and the impact they have had on the teaching profession. Updated in April 2011 to align with other national and state standards, the InTASC Model Core Teaching Standards now include standards not only for "beginning" teachers, but also for professionals. They set one standard for performance that will differ at various developmental stages of a teacher's career. "Another key point is that these standards maintain the delineation of knowledge, dispositions, and performances as a way to probe the complexity of the teacher's practice. The relationships among the three have been reframed, however, putting performance first—as the aspect that can be observed and assessed in teaching practice. The others were renamed. "'Essential knowledge' signals the role of declarative and procedural knowledge as necessary for effective practice, and 'critical dispositions'" indicates that habits of professional action and moral commitments that underlie the performances play a key role in how teachers do, in fact, act in practice" (Council of Chief State School Officers, 2011, p. 6). In reading over the actual standards, you will find that all areas that teachers need to develop are included. An abbreviated list of the 10 InTASC Model Core Teaching Standards are provided in the following chapter sections; a complete list, including performance, essential knowledge, and critical disposition expectations, are found in Appendix B or at www.ccsso.org/InTASC_Model_Core_Teaching_Standards_2011. pdf. It is important to read the entire document to see how the indicators provide examples of how a teacher might demonstrate each standard. The indicators are not intended as a checklist, but rather as a way to help you picture what each standard means.

InTASC Model Core Teaching Standards

■ Standard 1: Learner Development

The teacher understands how learners grow and develop, recognizing that patterns of learning and development vary individually within and across the cognitive, linguistic, social, emotional, and physical areas, and designs and implements developmentally appropriate and challenging learning experiences.

■ Standard 2: Learning Differences

The teacher uses understanding of individual differences and diverse cultures and communities to ensure inclusive learning environments that enable each learner to meet high standards.

■ Standard 3: Learning Environments

The teacher works with others to create environments that support individual and collaborative learning, encouraging positive social interaction, active engagement in learning, and self-motivation.

■ Standard 4: Content Knowledge

The teacher understands the central concepts, tools of inquiry, and structures of the discipline(s) he or she teaches and creates learning experiences that make the discipline accessible and meaningful for learners to assure mastery of the content to assure mastery of content.

■ Standard 5: Application of Content

The teacher understands how to connect concepts and use differing perspectives to engage learners in critical thinking, creativity, and collaborative problem solving related to authentic local and global issues.

■ Standard 6: Assessment

The teacher understands and uses multiple methods of assessment to engage learners in their own growth, to monitor learner progress, and to guide the teacher's and learner's decision making.

■ Standard 7: Planning for Instruction

The teacher plans instruction that supports every student in meeting rigorous learning goals by drawing upon knowlege of content areas, curriculum, cross-disciplinary skills, and pedagogy, as well as knowledge of learner and the community context.

■ Standard 8: Instructional Strategies

The teacher understands and uses a variety of instructional strategies to encourage learners to develop deep understanding of content areas and their connections, and to build skills to apply knowledge in meaningful ways.

■ Standard 9: Professional Learning and Ethical Practice

The teacher engages in ongoing professional learning and uses evidence to continually evaluate his or her practice, particularly the effects of his or her choices and actions on others (learners, families, other professionals, and the community), and adapts practice to meet the needs of each learner.

■ Standard 10: Leadership and Collaboration

The teacher seeks appropriate leadership roles and opportunities to take responsibility for student learning, to collaborate with learners, families, colleagues, other school professionals, and community members to ensure learner growth, and to advance the profession.

Figure 2-1 correlates the NAEYC Standards to the InTASC Model Core Teaching Standards. This may be a helpful tool as you continue to develop your portfolio because the indicators in both documents provide you with key information for writing satisfactory reflective narratives, which you will learn more about in Chapter 7.

NAEYC Standards for Early Childhood Professional Preparation Programs	InTASC Model Core Teaching Standard	InTASC Performance Indicators	InTASC Essential Knowledge Indicators	InTASC Critical Disposition Indicators
1. Promoting Child Development and Learning	1. Learner Development	1 (a–c)	1 (d–g)	1 (h–k)
2. Building Family and Community Relationships	1. Learner Development	1 (c)		1 (k)
	2. Learning Differences	2 (d)	2 (l, k)	2 (m)
	3. Learning Environments	3 (a, c, e, f)		3 (n)
	5. Application of Content			5 (n)
	6. Assessment			
	7. Planning for Instruction			7 (o)
	8. Instructional Strategies	8 (c, h, i)	8 (q)	8 (m)
	9. Professional Learning and Ethical Practice	9 (b)		9 (m)
	10. Leadership and Collaboration	10 (c, d, e, g, k)	10 (m)	10 (n, q)
3. Observing, Documenting and Assessing to Support Young Children and Families	1. Learner Development	1 (a, b)	1 (d–g)	1 (h, i, k)
	2. Learning Differences	2 (a–f), 2 (h)	2 (g, h, j, k)	2 (l, m. n, o)
	3. Learning Environments	3 (d, f)	3 (l)	
	4. Content Knowledge	4 (a, d, e, f, g)	4 (l, m)	4 (r)
	6. Assessment	6 (a–i)	6 (j–p)	6 (q–v)
	7. Planning for Instruction	7 (b, c, d, f)	7 (i–m)	7 (n, q)

FIGURE 2-1 *Comparison of NAEYC Standards for Early Childhood Professional Preparation Programs with InTASC Model Core Teaching Standards*

NAEYC Standards for Early Childhood Professional Preparation Programs	InTASC Model Core Teaching Standard	InTASC Performance Indicators	InTASC Essential Knowledge Indicators	InTASC Critical Disposition Indicators
	8. Instructional Strategies	8 (a, b, d, e, f)	8 (k)	8 (p, s)
	9. Professional Learning and Ethical Practice	9 (a, c, e)	9 (g–j)	9 (m)
	10. Leadership and Collaboration	10 (a, b)		
4. Using Developmentally Effective Approaches to Connect with Children and Families	1. Learner Development	1 (a, b)	1 (d–g)	1 (h, i, k)
	2. Learning Differences	2 (a–f), 2 (h)	2 (g, h, j, k)	2 (l–o)
	3. Learning Environments	3 (d, f, g, h)	3 (l)	3 (j, m)
	4. Content Knowledge	4 (a, d, e, f, g)	4 (l, m)	4 (r)
	5. Application of Content	5 (c)		5 (k, l)
	6. Assessment	6 (a–i)	6 (j–p)	6 (q–v)
	7. Planning for Instruction	7 (b, c, d, f)	7 (i–m)	7 (k, n, q)
	8. Instructional Strategies	8 (a, b, d, e, f, g)	8 (k, q, r)	8 (n, o, p, s)
	9. Professional Learning and Ethical Practice	9 (a, e, f)	9 (g–j)	9 (m)
	10. Leadership and Collaboration	10 (e, g)		10 (n)
5. Using Content Knowledge to Build Meaningful Curriculum	4. Content Knowledge	4 (a–i)	4 (j–n)	4 (o–r)
	5. Application of Content	5 (a–h)	T (i–p)	5 (q–s)
	6. Assessment	7 (a–f)	7 (g–m)	7 (n–q)
	7. Planning for Instruction	8 (a–i)	8 (j–o)	8 (p–s)
6. Becoming a Professional	4. Content Knowledge			4 (o, p, q)
	5. Application of Content			5 (q, r)
	6. Assessment	6 (a, c, g, i)	6 (j–p)	6 (t)

FIGURE 2-1   *Comparison of NAEYC Standards for Early Childhood Professional Preparation Programs with InTASC Model Core Teaching Standards (continued)*

NAEYC Standards for Early Childhood Professional Preparation Programs	InTASC Model Core Teaching Standard	InTASC Performance Indicators	InTASC Essential Knowledge Indicators	InTASC Critical Disposition Indicators
	7. Planning for Instruction		7 (f, k)	
	8. Instructional Strategies	8 (g)	8 (k, n, o)	8 (p)
	9. Professional Learning and Ethical Practice	9 (a–f)	9 (g–k)	9 (l–o)
	10. Leadership and Collaboration	10 (a–k)	10 (l–o)	10 (p–t)

FIGURE 2-1 *Comparison of NAEYC Standards for Early Childhood Professional Preparation Programs with InTASC Model Core Teaching Standards (continued)*

ACTIVITY 2-1

Take the time to generate a list of the activities an early childhood educator does throughout the school day. Items on your list probably include writing lesson plans, teaching various subjects, conferencing with parents, monitoring behavior, nursing wounds, motivating learners, and more. The list is endless and unique to each individual teacher and school setting.

ACTIVITY 2-2

Using the list you created, how could you verify your proficiency of each item? You may say you can write a good lesson plan, but how can you prove this? A well-designed, organized portfolio provides the "proof" that you are a competent teacher by the inclusion of concrete, tangible evidence, referred to as artifacts. (Artifacts will be defined and examined more closely in Chapter 6). Follow the example provided below and develop a possible artifact for each activity you listed in Step One.

Activity	Artifact	Other Possible Artifacts
Writing Lesson Plans	A detailed, well written plan	
Teaching Subject Matter	Supervisor's evaluation Self-evaluation Photographs of you teaching	
Conferencing with Parents	Letters Notes Emails to parents Parent conferences Behavior action plans	
Monitoring Behavior	Classroom rules Procedures Letters to families Classroom management plans Behavior action plans	
Nursing Wounds	Injury policies Procedures plan Reassuring songs or actions Self-reflection	
Motivating Learners	Lesson plans Classroom reward system Lesson motivators Lesson activators Classroom layout plan	

FIGURE 2-2   *Artifact Activity*

ACTIVITY 2-3

Think about the NAEYC standard under which each teacher activity and artifact would best fit. For example, a lesson plan could demonstrate your ability to make content meaningful. This would then demonstrate your knowledge of NAEYC Standard 5: Using Content Knowledge to Build Meaningful Curriculum. This same artifact would fall nicely under InTASC 4: Content Knowledge (d) "The teacher stimulates learner reflection on prior content knowledge, links new concepts to familiar concepts, and makes connections to learners' experiences" (Council of Chief State School Officers, 2011, p. 13).

A lesson plan could also be used to motivate young children. Then your artifact would be placed under NAEYC Standard 4: Using Developmentally Effective Approaches to Connect with Children and Families. It might also fit under InTASC 8: Instructional Strategies (n) The teacher knows how to use a wide variety of resources . . . to engage students in learning" (Council of Chief State School Officers, 2011, p. 1).

Figure 2-3 includes some examples of ideas for artifacts that match a given activity. Identify a possible NAEYC standard and an InTASC standard. The first one is done for you.

Activity	Artifact	NAEYC Standard	InTASC Standard
Lesson Plans	A detailed, well written plan	Standard 1c	Standard 7a
Conferencing with Parents	Behavior plan		
Monitoring Behavior	Classroom Rules		
Nursing Wounds	Injury Policies		
Motivating Learners	Classroom reward system		

FIGURE 2-3 Identifying Artifacts and Related INTASC Principle

ACTIVITY 2-4

Under what artifact, NAEYC standard, and InTASC standard would you place the activities listed in Figure 2-4? The first one is done for you. Add some of your own activities that you might include in your portfolio. Another way to process this information might be to create a table similar to Figure 2-4 . Using your course syllabi, decide if any of your class assignments could be viable artifacts; then align your course assignments with the NAEYC and InTASC standards.

Using Activities or Course Assignments to Identify Artifacts	Artifact	NAEYC Standard	InTASC Standard
Create a Dramatic Play Center	Plans and pictures of the dramatic play center. Include goals, objectives, directions, procedures, and assessments to document learning	1a: Knowing and understanding young children's characteristics and needs	7j: The teacher understands the strengths and needs of individual learners and how to plan instruction that is responsive to these strengths and needs
Plan a Tall Tale Study	Lesson Plan on *Babe the Blue Ox*		
Use an Assessment to Plan a Lesson	A pre-assessment to determine prior knowledge		
Attend a Professional Meeting	Agenda and notes from a meeting on Multiculturalism		
Communication with parents	A newsletter to parents describing the week's activities		

FIGURE 2-4 Using Activities or Course Assignments to Identify Artifacts

Summary

One powerful way to begin working with the NAEYC Standards and the InTASC Core Model Teaching Standards is by asking yourself, "What do teachers do?" You have learned that the NAEYC Standards are the accepted criteria used to demonstrate what a beginning early childhood teacher should know and do to be effective in the classroom. In early childhood education, the InTASC Core Model Teaching Standards are used to supplement NAEYC's specific areas by providing performance indicators, essential knowledge indicators, and critical disposition indicators. These guidelines of excellence and evidence help you see that you are becoming a successful emerging teacher. You have also seen how the two sets of standards are interrelated. Now you are ready to put this knowledge to work.

 ## Suggested Websites

The Council of Chief State School Officers website includes the new InTASC Principles and detailed explanations of them. Go to:

www.ccsso.org/InTASC_Model_Core_Teaching_Standards_2011.pdf.

The NAEYC website includes the new Standards for Early Childhood Professional Preparation Programs with detailed explanations. Go to:

www.naeyc.org.

 ## References

Council of Chief State School Officers. (2011, April). Interstate Teacher Assessment and Support Consortium (InTASC) Model Core Teaching Standards: A Resource for State Dialogue. Washington, DC: Author. Retrieved from www.ccsso.org/InTASC_Model_Core_Teaching_Standards_2011.pdf.

NAEYC Standards for Early Childhood Professional Preparation Programs. (2009). Position Statement. Retrieved from www.naeyc.org.

chapter 3

· ·

Electronic Portfolios

This chapter explains what electronic portfolios (e-portfolios) are, introduces you to the national technology standards for teachers, and discusses benefits and challenges associated with using e-portfolios. This chapter also discusses the skills and abilities you need to execute a successful e-portfolio, what hardware and software are necessary for your computer, and the recommended steps to start creating a successful e-portfolio. Finally, resources and a self-survey are provided to help you determine whether you are ready to develop your e-portfolio.

National Standards

In addition to NAEYC and InTASC standards, teacher candidates need to demonstrate mastery of technology standards and performance indicators as identified by the National Educational Technology Standards for Teachers (NETS-T). The NETS-T were developed by the International Society for Technology in Education (ISTE) in order to provide a framework for teachers as they "design, implement, and assess learning experiences to engage students and improve learning; enrich professional practice; and provide positive models for students, colleagues, and the community" (International Society for Technology in Education, 2008, p. 1). The full text of the NETS-T standards can be found at the ISTE website (www.iste.org/standards). Some states have also developed their own technology standards (e.g., see mttsonline.org/ for Maryland's Teacher Technology Standards). Teacher candidates who complete an e-portfolio also demonstrate competency in one or more of these areas, particularly standards/indicators 1a, 1d, 2a–c, 3a–d, 4, and 5b–d. While the 2010 InTASC principles do not have a separate standard for technology, it is understood that the ability to integrate technology in all areas of your planning, instruction, and assessment is critical. Choosing an e-portfolio over a traditional portfolio will demonstrate your technological skill to potential employers and will be helpful in your job search.

What Is an E-portfolio?

An e-portfolio is a multimedia collection that demonstrates your professional growth and development and your best work and proudest accomplishments during your teacher preparation period. E-portfolios (also known as digital portfolios, web portfolios, multimedia portfolios, and web folios) allow you to include a wide range of artifacts in various ways, including images, audio, video, documents, and hyperlinks to websites. These artifacts help provide evidence of your accomplishments as a teacher candidate (Barrett, 2007). Recent technological advances have encouraged initiatives for e-portfolios rather than print portfolios to document performance and learning (Buzzetto-More, 2010; Cambridge, Kahn, Tompkins, & Yancey, 2001; Hallam & Creagh, 2010; Milman, 1999). Many teacher preparation programs are turning to electronic portfolio systems to meet National Council of Accreditation of Teacher Education (NCATE) requirements (Barrett & Knezek, 2003; Young, 2002).

The advancing use and influence of technology in higher education have caused increasing numbers of institutions to use some form of electronic portfolios to evaluate teacher candidates (Carney, 2006; Ritzhaupt, Ndoye, & Parker, 2010). Some research shows that preservice teachers who capture information in the form of text, graphics, audio, and video produce a multimedia portrayal of their skills and accomplishments and are more apt to incorporate technology into their own classrooms (Barrett, 2001). The process of gathering and keeping track of information over time requires an organized approach to documentation and storage. The collection and archiving of student work can be facilitated by using a number of computer-based programs, ranging from spreadsheet applications that help organize student data (such as Microsoft Excel), to multimedia presentation software with portfolio applications (such as Keynote), to wikispaces (such as PBWorks), and to web-based programs (such as Task Stream). All of these applications have the potential to affect greatly the ways in which authentic assessment is used (Barrett, 2001).

What Are Some Benefits and Challenges to Creating an E-portfolio?

Creating an e-portfolio has many benefits. E-portfolios, like traditional paper portfolios, are used by preservice teachers to demonstrate their skills, competencies, and dispositions as they enter the professional field. However, e-portfolios are smaller and are easier to transport and access than are traditional paper portfolios. E-portfolios are inexpensive to duplicate and can be easily shared with others. Students who create e-portfolios have an opportunity to develop, and then showcase, their technological skills; in many cases, they learn new skills. Students who complete e-portfolios are also able to serve as mentors to others who may not feel as competent using technology in their practice. These students have greater flexibility and more options when selecting artifacts to include in the e-portfolio; such artifacts include animation, graphics, video, and sound (Ntuli, Keengwe, & Kyei-Blankson, 2009; Strudler & Wetzel, 2005; Wetzel & Strudler, 2005).

Another benefit of the e-portfolio is the ability to hyperlink to documents and websites. A hyperlink is a word or image in a document that a viewer can click on to move to another place in the document, to view another external document, or to view a webpage. Hyperlinking facilitates an easily modifiable and more flexible structure than is possible in print portfolios, and it allows easy and efficient navigation through the portfolio. The ability to include more types of information is paramount. Digital video of one's teaching performance, audio files of children reading, images of three-dimensional sculptures or constructions, scanned artifacts of student work, and text entries can all be included in the e-portfolio through hyperlinks. They each allow students to display the technical competence and familiarity with software applications that is now a necessary skill for teachers. Creativity, active learning, enhanced self-confidence, and dissemination to a broader community are other advantages of e-portfolios (Kilbane & Milman, 2003).

Just as there are benefits to creating e-portfolios, there are some challenges that you may encounter. One such challenge may be limited access to technology, both hardware and software. As we will discuss later in this chapter, you will need access to a computer that can properly store your materials and that is also current in terms of its software and processing speed. This is particularly important because the e-portfolio is likely to include high-quality images and video. The time that you spend developing your e-portfolio will be significant, especially if you do not already have requisite technological skills and competencies. You must also be ready to learn about new Web 2.0 tools that will enhance your e-portfolio, such as screen capture tools like Jing www.techsmith.com/jing/, or file-sharing websites like googledocs www.docs.google.com. It is also important that technical support be available in the event that you need assistance with troubleshooting.

What Hardware Do I Need to Create an Electronic Portfolio?

To create an electronic portfolio, you will need a computer with sufficient memory for storage, sufficient processing speed, video input and output ports, and any or all of the following drives: zip, CD-RW, or DV-RW (Pastore, 2010). In addition, you will need access to a printer, a flat-bed color scanner, a microphone, a digital still camera or digital video camera (if you plan to incorporate video clips), a CD burner (if you choose to publish your portfolio on a CD), a DVD burner (if you want to publish your portfolio on a DVD), and a flash or zip drive or other external drive for backup or transfer of digital assets. You can store your electronic portfolio on flash drives, CDs, DVDs, or on the Web as an html, PDF, Word, or PowerPoint file. Microsoft Word and PowerPoint files can be sent directly to the Web; however, if you plan to publish your portfolio on the Internet, you will need Internet service access. Any program that can create multimedia and/or webpages can be appropriate for electronic portfolios.

What Software Can I Use to Create an Electronic Portfolio?

On a basic level, any tool that allows you to design and publish digital content can be used for e-portfolios. Some popular programs for creating materials suitable for e-portfolios include:

- Microsoft SharePoint Designer: This is a program designed to integrate external data, control customization of layout, and edit the website.
- Apple iMovie or Windows Live MovieMaker: Both programs allow video creation and editing using images, video, text, and music.

- Microsoft Office Suite (Microsoft Word, Microsoft PowerPoint, Microsoft Excel): These desktop applications are designed for word processing, presentations, and spreadsheets, respectively. This suite was created for computers that use Windows operating systems.
- Apple iWork Office Suite (Apple Pages, Apple Keynote, Apple Numbers): These desktop applications are designed for word processing, presentations, and spreadsheets. This suite was created for computers that use MAC operating systems.
- Clip art and digital photos
- Adobe Creative Suite: Design, editing, and website development applications
- E-portfolio online management systems:
  - Chalk & Wire, chalkandwire.com/index.php/product/overview
  - TaskStream, www.taskstream.com/pub/e-Portfolios.asp?ReferringPage=1
- Wiki: Wikispaces are community websites to which anyone can contribute content. Permissions may be changed so that access and editing privileges are limited. Wikispaces are becoming increasingly popular among educators as an alternative to creating a traditional website. Students are also using wikispaces for e-portfolios. Popular wikispace sites include:
  - Wikispaces: www.wikispaces.com/
  - PBWorks: pbworks.com/
  - WetPaint: wikisineducation.wetpaint.com/
- Dr. Helen Barrett, the Educational Technology Coordinator for the School of Education, University of Alaska Anchorage, maintains electronicportfolios.com/portfolios.html, which has a rich collection of web resources on alternative assessment and electronic portfolios.

What Should I Think about As I Develop an E-portfolio?

There is no one right way to create an e-portfolio; however, there are some things that you should keep in mind .. When you prepare your electronic portfolio, you will follow a process similar to creating a traditional paper portfolio (highlighted in other chapters of this book). In addition, consider the following when creating the e-portfolio:

1. Become technologically organized. You should get organized and stay organized. Create folders on your computer where you will store your electronic artifacts. Give those folders names that have meaning (such as "Teaching Video Clips"), and give the electronic artifacts meaningful names (such as "Mathematics, Gr. 3, 10-2012"). Decide on a consistent schedule to add and organize those artifacts and folders. Then create a backup copy! Flash drives break, CDs snap, and computers crash. Always have two sets of documentation. This is critically important.
2. Know (or learn) the technology, both hardware and software. You will need to explore different tools in order to create your e-portfolio. You must understand how to use these tools to polish your artifacts and to use them most effectively in the e-portfolio. If you do not understand the technology, ask for help. For example, you may have a video clip of a 30-minute science lesson. Do you know how to transfer that clip from the camcorder to your computer? Do you know how to use video-editing tools to shorten that clip so that the portfolio reviewer only sees the most meaningful part of your lesson?

3. Digitize your work. This tip addresses both the technology and your organizational skills. Some artifacts and supporting materials will need to be transformed into a digital format. Do you have access to equipment to do this? If you do, do you know how to use the equipment? If you do not, do you know where to go in order to gain access? Do not wait until the last minute. Digitize artifacts and supporting materials regularly.

4. Be creative, but conservative. One benefit of using e-portfolios is that you are able to show off your creativity and your technological skills. Take advantage of the opportunity by making the most of the available options. Keep in mind, however, that you should not let the "bells and whistles" overshadow the content of your e-portfolio.

5. Make sure it all works. Before you share your final e-portfolio with a reviewer, check and recheck each section of your e-portfolio. Be sure that any links to external websites are still active and that all hyperlinks to documents within the e-portfolio open properly.

ACTIVITY 3-1

Self-Survey

Ask yourself the following questions. The answers that you provide should give you insight about whether you are prepared to begin your e-portfolio or whether you need more support. If you think you need more support, contact faculty members who have worked with students on e-portfolios. You can also consult websites dedicated to supporting teachers who want to create e-portfolios (see the Web resources already mentioned in this chapter).

1. Do I know how to use a computer?	YES	NO
2. Am I able to use my computer or tablet to accomplish this task? That is, does my computer or tablet have sufficient memory and processing speed in order to handle my e-portfolio?	YES	NO
3. Am I comfortable using a variety of software programs (e.g., Microsoft Word, PPT, and Excel)?	YES	NO
4. Am I able to use hardware to acquire materials that will be useful in the development of my e-portfolio? For example, am I able to capture a teaching episode with a digital video camera, edit that video by trimming unwanted footage, and upload the trimmed clip to my e-portfolio?	YES	NO
5. Do I understand the basics regarding embedding files and hyperlinking to documents and/or websites?	YES	NO
6. Do I have access to the necessary resources in order to develop my e-portfolio (e.g., computer, camcorder, scanner, technology support)?	YES	NO
7. Am I interested in exploring new technologies in order to fully develop my e-portfolio?	YES	NO
8. Am I easily frustrated when computers don't perform the way that I want them to?	YES	NO

Summary

Basically, creating an e-portfolio involves the processes of both portfolio development and multimedia development. E-portfolios require a certain level of technical skill, access to technical support, and access to relevant hardware and software. Helpful hints and good advice can come primarily from individuals who have developed electronic portfolios. Both paper and electronic portfolios involve collecting materials, selecting materials, and reflecting on the materials; they merely differ in how they are produced. The steps for developing materials that can be used in both an e-portfolio and a traditional portfolio will be discussed more fully later in the text.

 ## Suggested Websites

Maryland's technology standards:

mttsonline.org/

Web tools that will enhance your e-portfolio:

www.techsmith.com/jing/

File-sharing websites like googledocs:

docs.google.com

E-portfolios online management systems:

chalkandwire.com/index.php/product/overvierview

www.taskstream.com/pub/e-Portfolios.asp? ReferringPage=1

Popular wikispace sites:

www.wikispaces.com/

pbworks.com/

wikisineducation.wetpaint.com/

Web resources:

electronicsportfolios.com/portfolios.html

Ball State University Teachers College, Teacher Education Electronic Portfolio website:

portfolio.iweb.bsu.edu/default.html

Iowa State University, Teacher Education Program website:

www.teacher.hs.iastate.edu/eportfolio.php

Penn State University:

portfolio.psu.edu/2009/11/why-have-an-e-portfolio. html

Pastore, R. S. (2010). Webportfolio.info information website

webportfolio.info/

 ## References

Barrett, H. (2001). Electronic portfolios = multimedia development + portfolio development: The electronic portfolio development process. In B. L. Cambridge, S. Kahn, D. P. Tompkins, & K. B. Yancey (Eds.), *Electronic portfolios* (pp. 110–116). Washington, DC: American Association for Higher Education.

Barrett, H. C. (2007). Researching electronic portfolios and learner engagement: The REFLECT initiative. *Journal of Adolescent & Adult Literacy, 50*(6), 436–449.

Barrett, H., & Knezek, D. (2003, April). *E-portfolios: Issues in assessment and preservice teacher preparation.* Paper presented at the Annual Conference of the American Educational Research Association, Chicago, IL.

Buzzetto-More, N. (2010). Assessing the efficacy and effectiveness of an e-portfolio used for summative assessment. *Interdisciplinary Journal of E-Learning and Learning Objects, 6*(20), 61–85.

Cambridge, B. L., Kahn, S., Tompkins, D. P., & Yancey, K. B. (Eds.) (2001). *Electronic portfolios: Emerging practices in student, faculty, and institutional learning.* Washington, DC: American Association for Higher Education.

Carney, J. (2006). Analyzing research on teachers' electronic portfolios: What does it tell us about portfolios and methods for studying them? *Journal of Computing in Teacher Education, 22*(3). 89–99.

Hallam, G., & Creagh, T. (2010). ePortfolio use by students in Australia: A review of the Australian ePortfolio project. *Higher Education Research & Development, 29*(2), 179–193.

International Society for Technology in Education. (2008). *National educational technology standards for teachers.* Eugene, OR: Author.

Kilbane, C. R., & Milman, N. (2003). *The digital teaching portfolio handbook.* Upper Saddle River, NJ: Pearson.

Milman, N. (1999). Web-based electronic teaching portfolios for preservice teachers. In *Proceedings of Society for Information Technology and Teacher Education International Conference.* 1174–1179, Chesapeake, VA: AACE.

Ntuli, E., Keengwe, J., & Kyei-Blankson, L. (2009). Electronic portfolios in teacher education: A case study of early childhood teacher candidates. *Early Childhood Education Journal, 37,* 121–126.

Pastore, R. S. (2010). Webportfolio.info@Teacherworldcom. [Online]. http://webportfoliol.info/ Retrieved November 2, 2011.

Ritzhaupt, A. D., Ndoye, A., & Parker, M. A. (2010). Validation of the electronic portfolio student perspective instrument (EPSPI): Conditions under a different integration initiative. *Journal of Digital Learning in Teacher Education, 26*(3), 111–119.

Strudler, N., & Wetzel, K. (2005). The diffusion of electronic portfolios in teacher education: Issues of initiation and implementation. *Journal of Research on Technology in Education, 37*(4), 411–433.

Wetzel, K., & Strudler, N. (2005). The diffusion of electronic portfolios in teacher education: Next steps and recommendations from accomplished users. *Journal of Research on Technology in Education, 38*(2), 231–243.

Young, J. R. (2002). 'E-portfolios' could give students a new sense of their accomplishments. *Chronicle of Higher Education, 48*(26), A31–A32.

chapter 4

Setting Up Your Portfolio

Portfolios are publications, like books and magazines. The more appealing they are, the better chance they have of being read and taken seriously (Jones & Shelton, 2006). To be effective, your portfolio needs to have a well-established organizational system that makes sense to you and that you can explain to other educators. You already know that a portfolio in early childhood education will be organized around standards that are used by your university and that represent your understanding of young children and their families. In this book, we use the National Association for the Education of Young Children (NAEYC) standards because these are the standards that govern our field of early childhood education (www.naeyc.org). We have also used the InTASC p standards because these are the principles required by the National Council for the Accreditation of Teacher Education (NCATE) for accreditation. "NCATE accreditation is a mark of distinction, and provides recognition that the college of Education has met national professional standards for the preparation of teachers" (www.ccsso.org/intasc.html).

Traditional portfolios are published on paper, but a recent advancement in the field of portfolio development is the electronic portfolio, which was discussed in Chapter 3. With either type of portfolio, the organization will be similar. "Traditional portfolios are simpler to use when you wish to display hard copies of certain artifacts or create smaller portable portfolios, [but] in terms of organization and storage, the accumulation of all your artifacts can quickly become . . . unwieldy" (Rieman & Okrasinski, 2007, p. 25). Electronic portfolios also involve multimedia expertise.

Organization of the Traditional Paper Portfolio

A traditional paper portfolio is usually contained in an extra-wide or extended 3-inch three-ring binder, preferably in white, black, or blue. Extra-wide dividers designate each section, which assists with management. To access materials within each section, extra-wide tabs should be used. These, like the extended binder and dividers, can be purchased at most office supply stores or online. Artifacts should be contained in sheet protectors.

Outside and Inside Cover Pages

The portfolio should be personalized with identical outside and inside cover pages, that include the title, your (the preparer's) name, your major, and the name of your college or university (see Figure 4-1).

PROFESSIONAL PORTFOLIO

EARLY CHILDHOOD EDUCATION

XYZ UNIVERSITY

YOUR NAME

FIGURE 4-1 *Outside and Inside Cover Page*

Table of Contents

As in any book, the table of contents organizes the evidence you wish to display. The table of contents should be a directory of all the documents included in your portfolio, listed in the order that they appear within the portfolio. For example, under NAEYC 1, Promoting Child Development and Learning, you would list all artifacts in the order that they appear within the document. It is wise to avoid numbering items or pages because the artifacts may be constantly changing. It may also be wise to wait to complete your table of contents until your final showcase portfolio is nearing completion. Figure 4-2 is an illustration of a typical table of contents.

Table of Contents

I. Personal Background
- Acceptance letter to the University
- Official Transcript from the University
- Praxis I Test Scores
- Acceptance letter to the Early Childhood Education Program
- Autobiography
- Philosophy of Education
- Dean's List Letters
- Kappa Delta Pi Certificate
- Criminal Background Clearance
- Resume

II. Professional Background

NAEYC 1-Promoting Child Development and Learning
- Child Case Study
- Developmentally Appropriate Practice Activity Packets
- Dramatic Play Box
- Child Case Study
- Hyperlexia Research Paper

NAEYC 2-Building Family and Community Relationships
- Service Learning Project
- Action Research Project
- IEP Reflection and Action Plan
- Field Trip Plan
- Family Conference Ideas
- Samples of Letters to Families
- Family Literacy Bag

NAEYC 3-Observing, Documenting and Assessing to Support Young Children and Families
- Cycle of Learning Lesson Plan
- Phonological Awareness Project
- Child Case Study
- Assessment Plans

FIGURE 4-2   *Table of Contents*

FIGURE 4-2 *Table of Contents (continued)*

Philosophy Statement

Following the table of contents, you will lay the foundation for your portfolio with a thoughtful, well-written philosophy statement. Your philosophy statement is a concise, well-written statement that details your beliefs and values related to teaching, learning, and young children. It represents you and the ideals to which you aspire, and connects theory to practice. In the next chapter we will look more carefully at your personal and professional educational philosophy, and include examples of excellent philosophy statements written by college students.

Primary Sections of Your Portfolio

The portfolio is divided into three main sections: Section I: Personal Background; Section II: Professional Background; and Section III: Appendix. Each section should begin with a page that identifies that portion of the portfolio.

■ Section I: Personal Background

As you can see from the table of contents, the personal background section provides a glimpse of who you as a preservice teacher and offers a profile of your background and experiences. You should ask: Who am I? What is important for others to know about me? What experiences have I had that will demonstrate my readiness to teach? A list of items that might be in your personal background section are listed and detailed below.

The personal background section often begins with an autobiography—a two- to three-page "story" of you as a preservice teacher. Include something about yourself, your family background, your interests and hobbies. The most important part of the story comprises why you decided to become an educator of young children. What qualities do you possess that will enhance your qualifications as a teacher? What were some early experiences that influenced your decision to teach and how you plan to teach? What are some central ideas about teaching and learning that will influence your development as an emerging teacher?

Other items that may be included in the personal background section include:

- Letter of introduction
- Resume
- University transcript(s) from all higher education institutions attended
- PRAXIS I and II scores
- Speech and hearing screening results
- Letter of acceptance into an early childhood education program or other program
- Letters of recommendation
- Work experience documents
- Honors, awards, and special recognition
- Membership certificates or cards
- Certificates of participation in workshops or conferences
- Documentation of any special skills
- Documentation of volunteer work

This list is not intended to be exhaustive, and you may have additional items that you want to include.

■ Section II: Professional Background

This section is the heart and soul of the portfolio! This is where your portfolio becomes a true professional document and not a scrapbook because it contains a record of quantitative and qualitative growth over time under each standard. Section II provides artifacts that demonstrate your knowledge of professional standards and reflects your growth and development. This section of artifacts actually helps you better understand teaching as a profession, gain greater self-understanding, and capture the complexities of teaching.

Following the Section II identification page, there should be a complete list of the six NAEYC Standards and the 10 InTASC Standards (see Figures 4-3 and 4-4). If you are using another set of standards, it is recommended that they, too, be listed in their entirety. Each of the six NAEYC Standards or alternative defining standards should have its own title page and corresponding labeled tab because these are the main subheadings in Section II If you are using two sets of standards, we recommend including the corresponding standard on the title page as well. Your university may have its own policy about standards as dividing pages.

STANDARD 1. PROMOTING CHILD DEVELOPMENT AND LEARNING
Candidates prepared in early childhood degree programs are grounded in a child development knowledge base. They use their understanding of young children's characteristics and needs, and of multiple interacting influences on children's development and learning, to create environments that are healthy, respectful, supportive, and challenging for each child.

STANDARD 2. BUILDING FAMILY AND COMMUNITY RELATIONSHIPS
Candidates prepared in early childhood degree programs understand that successful early childhood education depends upon partnerships with children's families and communities. They know about, understand, and value the importance and complex characteristics of children's families and communities. They use this understanding to create respectful, reciprocal relationships that support and empower families, and to involve all families in their children's development and learning.

STANDARD 3. OBSERVING, DOCUMENTING, AND ASSESSING TO SUPPORT YOUNG CHILDREN AND FAMILIES
Candidates prepared in early childhood degree programs understand that child observation, documentation, and other forms of assessment are central to the practice of all early childhood professionals. They know about and understand the goals, benefits, and uses of assessment. They know about and use systematic observations, documentation, and other effective assessment strategies in a responsible way, in partnership with families and other professionals, to positively influence the development of every child.

STANDARD 4. USING DEVELOPMENTALLY EFFECTIVE APPROACHES
Candidates prepared in early childhood degree programs understand that teaching and learning with young children is a complex enterprise, and its details vary depending on children's ages, characteristics, and the settings within which teaching and learning occur. They understand and use positive relationships and supportive interactions as the foundation for their work with young children and families. Candidates know, understand, and use a wide array of developmentally appropriate approaches, instructional strategies, and tools to connect with children and families and positively influence each child's development and learning.

STANDARD 5. USING CONTENT KNOWLEDGE TO BUILD MEANINGFUL CURRICULUM
Candidates prepared in early childhood degree programs use their knowledge of academic disciplines to design, implement, and evaluate experiences that promote positive development and learning for each and every young child. Candidates understand the importance of developmental domains and academic (or content) disciplines in early childhood curriculum. They know the essential concepts, inquiry tools, and structure of content areas, including academic subjects, and can identify resources to deepen their understanding. Candidates use their own knowledge and other resources to design, implement, and evaluate meaningful, challenging curriculum that promotes comprehensive developmental and learning outcomes for every young child.

STANDARD 6. BECOMING A PROFESSIONAL
Candidates prepared in early childhood degree programs identify and conduct themselves as members of the early childhood profession. They know and use ethical guidelines and other professional standards related to early childhood practice. They are continuous, collaborative learners who demonstrate knowledgeable, reflective and critical perspectives on their work, making informed decisions that integrate knowledge from a variety of sources. They are informed advocates for sound educational practices and policies.

FIGURE 4-3 List of the NAEYC Standards (2010)
Source: www.naeyc.org.

Standard #1: Learner Development. The teacher understands how learners grow and develop, recognizing that patterns of learning and development vary individually within and across the cognitive, linguistic, social, emotional, and physical areas, and designs and implements developmentally appropriate and challenging learning experiences.

Standard #2: Learning Differences. The teacher uses understanding of individual differences and diverse cultures and communities to ensure inclusive learning environments that enable each learner to meet high standards.

Standard #3: Learning Environments. The teacher works with others to create environments that support individual and collaborative learning.

Standard #4: Content Knowledge. The teacher understands the central concepts, tools of inquiry, and structures of the discipline(s) he or she teaches and creates learning experiences that make the discipline accessible and meaningful for learners to assure mastery of the content.

Standard #5: Application of Content. The teacher understands how to connect concepts and use differing perspectives to engage learners in critical thinking, creativity, and collaborative problem solving related to authentic local and global issues.

Standard #6: Assessment. The teacher understands and uses multiple methods of assessment to engage learners in their own growth, to monitor learner progress, and to guide the teacher's and learner's decision making.

Standard #7: Planning for Instruction. The teacher plans instruction that supports every student in meeting rigorous learning goals by drawing upon knowledge of content areas, curriculum, cross-disciplinary skills, and pedagogy, as well as knowledge of learners and the community context.

Standard #8: Instructional Strategies. The teacher understands and uses a variety of instructional strategies to encourage learners to develop deep understanding of content areas and their connections, and to build skills to apply knowledge in meaningful ways.

Standard #9: Professional Learning and Ethical Practice. The teacher engages in ongoing professional learning and uses evidence to continually evaluate his/her practice, particularly the effects of his/her choices and actions on others (learners, families, other professionals, and the community), and adapts practice to meet the needs of each learner.

Standard #10: Leadership and Collaboration. The teacher seeks appropriate leadership roles and opportunities to take responsibility for student learning, to collaborate with learners, families, colleagues, other school professionals, and community members to ensure learner growth, and to advance the profession.

FIGURE 4-4   *List of InTASC Model Core Teaching Standards*
Source: http://www.ccsso.org/intasc.

As you begin organizing Section II, the professional background section of your portfolio, you will begin with a whole-page section break, stating, "Section II: Professional Background." How this section is divided depends upon the standards used by your college or university. Many schools with early childhood education programs use the NAEYC standards to provide the divisions because this organization is the accrediting agent for early childhood. In this case, there will be six (6) divisions in Section II, one for each of the NAEYC Standards. See Figure 4-5 for an example of how this would look.

> ### NAEYC STANDARD 1
>
> ### PROMOTING CHILD DEVELOPMENT
>
> ### AND LEARNING
>
> Candidates prepared in early childhood degree programs are grounded in a child development knowledge base. They use their understanding of young children's characteristics and needs, and of multiple interacting influences on children's development and learning, to create environments that are healthy, respectful, supportive, and challenging for each child.
>
> **Key elements of Standard 1**
>
> **1a:** Knowing and understanding young children's characteristics and needs, from birth through age 8.
>
> **1b:** Knowing and understanding the multiple influences on early development and learning
>
> **1c:** Using developmental knowledge to create healthy, respectful, supportive, and challenging learning environments for young children

FIGURE 4-5 *Standard Title Page for NAEYC Standards*
Source: Printed with permission from NAEYC.

Some universities that are accredited by NCATE expect students to use the InTASC standards. In this case, the portfolio will have 10 divisions, one for each of the InTASC Standards. See Figure 4-6 for a sample division page using the InTASC format. Still other institutions may require students to use both the InTASC and NAEYC standards. A sample of that format is illustrated in Figure 4-7.

The heading for each artifact includes the title stating what the artifact is. The heading can include the course number and/or the title of the course, as well as the semester

> # InTASC Standard 1:
> # Learner Development
>
> The teacher understands how children learn and develop, recognizing that patterns of learning and development vary individually within and across the cognitive, linguistic, social, emotional, and physical areas, and designs and implements developmentally appropriate and challenging learning experiences.

FIGURE 4-6 *Standard Title Page for InTASC Model Core Teaching Standards*
Source: Printed with permission from CCSSO.

NAEYC Standard 1

Promoting Child Development and Learning

Candidates prepared in early childhood degree programs are grounded in a child development knowledge base. They use their understanding of young children's characteristics and needs, and of multiple interacting influences on children's development and learning, to create environments that are healthy, respectful, supportive, and challenging for each child.

InTASC Principle 1:
Learner Development
The teacher understands how children learn and develop, recognizing that patterns of learning and development vary individually within and across the cognitive, linguistic, social, emotional, and physical areas, and designs and implements developmentally appropriate and challenging learning experiences.

FIGURE 4-7 *Standard Title Page for both NAEYC and InTASC Standards*
Source: Printed with permission from NAEYC and CCSSO.

the artifact was completed (see the example in Figure 4-8). Also include the standard and the key elements of that standard. Figure 4-8 shows what is meant by the NAEYC standard and its key elements, and by the InTASC standard and the letter of the performance, essential knowledge, or critical disposition used to describe your artifact.

Following this heading is your narrative, which is written in type that is at least 12 points and uses 1.15, 1.5, or 2.0 spacing so that it does not look crowded and is very readable. Try to keep it to one page if at all possible.

Artifacts that support the identified NAEYC and InTASC standard(s) follow the division page. What artifacts are and how they provide evidence of the standards will be discussed later in the text. At this stage, you should collect as many artifacts as possible. In your final portfolio, you should aim for three to five high-quality artifacts under each standard.

Read Aloud

ECED 360

Spring 2011

NAEYC Standard #1c: Promoting Child Development and Learning (c) Using developmental knowledge to create healthy, respectful, supportive, and challenging learning environments.

InTASC Standard #8n: Instructional Strategies (n)The teacher knows when and how to use appropriate strategies to differentiate instruction and engage all students in complex thinking and meaningful tasks.

FIGURE 4-8 *Example of Artifact Heading*

■ Section III: Appendix

The appendix is a collection of supplementary materials that are valued by you but are not related directly to an identified competency or standard. For clarity, items in the appendix should be supported by a caption. These items do not need to be accompanied by a reflective narrative. Items in the appendix can include photographs, lengthy papers, letters from parents of students, and memorabilia that is not closely linked to a specific artifact. Items in the appendix should be listed in the table of contents in the order in which they appear in your portfolio.

ACTIVITY 4-1

Begin setting up your portfolio. For a paper portfolio, buy a 3-inch extra-wide binder with extra-wide dividers. With either a paper or electronic portfolio, first designate your three main sections. Design your inside and outside cover page. Then begin formatting your title pages using the standards that your college or university prefers.

Summary

The organization of the portfolio is critical to the management and accessibility of artifacts and documents. Using three main sections is a logical way to organize items. Artifacts that describe who you are are placed in the personal background section. Items that show what you know and have learned are located in the professional section. The professional seciton will be the bulk of your portfolio. The NAEYC and/or InTASC standards are used as subheadings in the professional background section. Each standard has a title page, followed by reflective narratives and artifacts that document your growth as an emerging teacher. Supporting items of interest go in the appendix.

 ## Suggested Websites

Portfolio guidelines from various universities' colleges of education can be found at:

http://ftad.osu.edu/portfolio/into.html

http://reach.ucf.edu/~ed_found/gpi.html

http://faculty.weber.edu/vnapper/portfolios/Prtflns.htm

http://ftad.osu._edu/portfolio.into.html

 ## References

Council of Chief State School Officers. (2011, April). Interstate Teacher Assessment and Support Consortium (InTASC) Model Core Teaching Standards: A resource for state dialogue. Washington, DC: Author.

Jones, M., & Shelton, M. (2006). *Developing your portfolio: Enhancing your learning and showing your stuff: A guide for the early childhood student or professional.* New York: Routledge.

NAEYC Standards for Early Childhood Professional Preparation Programs. (2009). Position Statement. Retrieved from www.naeyc.org.

Rieman, P. L., & Okrasinski, J. (2007). *Creating your teaching portfolio* (2nd ed.). Boston: McGraw Hill.

chapter 5

Developing Your Philosophy of Education Statement

A philosophy of education is a personal statement of your purpose, process, dispositions, and ideals of teaching. Your philosophy also describes your personal attitudes toward teaching. As a preservice intern beginning the exciting process of working with young children and their families, it's important to reflect on your beliefs and attitudes as they pertain to young children and your role as their teacher. Look at your philosophy of education as a work in process, growing and changing as you grow and change. In this chapter, we will identify why *a philosophy of education is important and* where *it should be placed in your portfolio. We will end by offering suggestions about* how *to write your philosophy of education statement.*

Where Does My Philosophy Come From?

When asking preservice interns why they want to enter the teaching profession, the answers are deeply personal and varied. Many students express how much they love children, how they have played teacher to their unsuspecting siblings, and how they have always known that this field of work is their passion. Other students share stories of teachers they had in elementary school, both good and bad. As we ask you to probe deeper and elaborate more fully on what you like specifically about working with young children, your individual attitudes, beliefs, and ideals will begin to emerge. It is important to examine your personal beliefs to help frame how you want to interact with young children and their families. It will help you become a better teacher, with a clear direction of where you're going and how you want to get there.

It is recommended that you begin a philosophy of education early in your preservice training and make changes to it as your work and experience with young children strengthens. Even in your first early childhood course, you should try to develop a philosophy of education statement. Take the time to reflect on why you're entering the field of early childhood education and what personal attitudes and beliefs you hold. Examine your knowledge, background, prior and present experiences, observations, and discussions with early childhood professionals to assist you in determining what you hold to be important. How will this affect the lives of young children? As you take additional courses and engage in more fieldwork, you will be exposed to early childhood from a historical perspective and learn that the education of preschool-age children "has proven to be an extremely important component of the total educational system" (Roopnarine & Johnson, 2005, p. 12). New ideas, theories of child development, and principles you will be learning about in your coursework build a helpful framework to guide and strengthen your philosophy of education statement.

Your philosophy of education evolves as you learn more and more about child development and learning theories. Reflecting on the major theories of early childhood education is an effective method to help you start writing a personal philosophy of education statement. Review the major learning theories in Figure 5-1 and identify the components that best exemplify your attitudes and beliefs.

Learning Theory	Basic Tenets of the Theory	Major Theorists
Basic needs theory	The hierarchy of humans' basic needs is often depicted as a pyramid consisting of five levels; higher needs can only be met if the lower ones are satisfied. Needs include physiological, safety, love/belonging, esteem, and self-actualization-self-transcendence.	Maslow (1908–1970)
Behaviorism and social learning theory	Behaviorism uses stimuli and responses, classical and operant conditioning, to develop behavior. Social learning theory emphasizes the role of modeling in developing behavior.	Skinner (1904–1990) Pavlov (1849–1936) Bandura (1977–) Watson (1878–1958)
Cognitive-developmental theory	A theory that views children as actively constructing knowledge as they manipulate and explore their world; cognitive development takes place in stages.	Piaget (1896–1980)
Dynamic structuralism	An alternative to Piaget's theory, the neo-nativism movement eliminates structure in stages. Instead, common human genetics is dynamic, branching out in many directions. Each strand represents a potential area of skills within the major domains of child development—physical, cognitive, and social/emotional.	Fischer (1943–)
Ecological systems theory	Child's heredity joins with multiple levels of the surrounding environment, from microsystems to macrosystems, to form development, patterns, relationships, personalities, and capacities.	Bronfenbrenner (1917–2005)
Ethological theory of attachment	A theory that views infant–caregiver bonding as necessary for feelings of security and the capacity to form trusting relationships.	Bowlby (1907–1990)

FIGURE 5-1 *Summary of Early Childhood Learning Theories*
Source: Berk, 2006; Crain, 2000; Puckett & Black, 2005.

Learning Theory	Basic Tenets of the Theory	Major Theorists
Information processing theory	In 1968 Atkinson and Shiffrin proposed an approach that views the human mind as a symbol-manipulating system through which information flows; cognitive development is a continuous process.	Atkinson (1929–) Klahr (1939–)& MacWhinney (1945–)
Maturation theory	Based on evolutionary ideas, child development was seen as a genetically determined series of events that unfold automatically.	Hall (1844–1924); Gesell (1880–1961)
Moral development	Kohlberg's six stages explain the development of moral reasoning; they emerge from children's own think- ing about moral problems, and are the basis for ethical behavior. Gilligan, critical of Kohlberg, based her theory on inter- relationships of ethics, care, and compassion.	Kohlberg (1927–1987) Gilligan (1936–)
Montessori's educa- tional philosophy	Children learn on their own, and quite differently from adults. Her theory includes five sensitive periods: for order, for details, for the use of hands, for walking, and for language, and puts faith in Nature's laws guiding the child through child-centered education.	Montessori (1870–1952)
Multiple intelligence theory	This theory proposes at least eight independent intelli- gences based on distinct sets of processing operations that allow individuals to engage in a wide range of culturally valued activities.	Gardner (1943–)
Psychosocial theory	Expands on Freud's theory, emphasizing psychosocial outcomes at each of eight stages of development. Personal- ity, attitudes, and skill development help children become active members of their society.	Erikson (1902–1994)
Sociocultural theory	Children acquire ways of thinking and behaving that come from a community's culture and from cooperative experi- ences with adults or more experienced peers.	Vygotsy (1896–1934)

FIGURE 5-1   *Summary of Early Childhood Learning Theories (continued)*

A clearly written philosophy statement not only helps you as a reflective practi-tioner in the field of early childhood education, it can also assist in the employment process. Upon graduation, a philosophy statement of education is an important docu-ment. It identifies your belief as a novice teacher, and it can be valuable in the promo-tion and tenure process. In a competitive marketplace, your philosophy of education statement can help set you apart from the competition and provide school person-nel with a clear understanding of who you are as an educator. Although this state-ment covers numerous issues, it must be very concise. Usually philosophy statements are only one page in length. While the writing can vary, a straightforward narrative approach is recommended. The best way to articulate your passion for teaching and children is through a meaningful, genuine, and clearly written philosophy of educa-tion statement.

Where Does My Philosophy Statement Belong?

The philosophy of education statement is the first document in your portfolio. It is the first item read by portfolio assessors and potential employers. The philosophy of education creates a starting point, but it leaves a lasting impression. It should be concise, clearly written, and true to your identity as an early childhood educator. You will be judged on your written expression; sentence structure; and ability to communicate your thoughts, attitudes, and beliefs about teaching. As you write, keep your audience in mind and abstain from controversial or political comments that may offend readers. For example, if you feel that all mothers should stay at home raising their young children, and you're presenting your portfolio to a working mother, this attitude is best left out of your philosophy of education statement. This reminder may sound obvious, but it's been done!

How Do I Develop a Philosophy Statement?

How can I develop a philosophy of education statement when my experience working with young children is limited? This is a question frequently asked by preservice interns early in their careers. For many of you, your experience working with young children is limited to babysitting or assisting in a classroom. You do have many years as a student, however, and you know what you like and dislike about your classroom experiences as a learner. The following questions can help get you started:

- Why do I want to become an early childhood educator?
- What are the roles and responsibilities of a good teacher?
- What are my beliefs about how children learn?
- What methods of teaching are most effective?
- What are the qualities of an excellent teacher?
- How is student learning and potential maximized effectively?
- What is my view of the role of the family and community in teaching?
- What theories or philosophies support my ideas?
- Why is teaching an important career?
- What are the obstacles facing children and families and how can I help them overcome these obstacles? (http://resumes-for-teachers).

Spend time thinking about these questions and record some ideas. Your philosophy of education statement will begin to emerge as you reflect on your experiences as a teacher and learner.

Strategies to Get You Started

An effective starting point for many preservice teachers is to find a meaningful quote that exemplifies your beliefs about teaching and young children. Then explain in the body of your philosophy your answers to the questions already listed in this chapter. Spend time researching quotes and determine if there is one of particular personal meaning. Some may find it easier to express their beliefs in the form of a poem, while others may use a bullet format to express their values in concise and brief statements. Your college or university department of education should have a conceptual framework or philosophy guiding coursework and experiences. Reading and understanding this document can give you ideas for your personal philosophy statement. Take the time to be reflective, and you'll be surprisingly pleased with the results!

Philosophy of Education and Reflective Practice

As stated earlier, a philosophy of education statement is a work in progress, growing and changing as you gain experience, increased commitment, and understanding of the field of early childhood education. Make sure you continue to reflect on your statement throughout your work as a preservice teacher. The philosophy of education statement you write as a freshman in college will most likely not be the same that you use during your portfolio presentation as a senior. You may find that your beliefs change as you work in the field, and your philosophy should change as well. Continue to reflect on your experiences and make the necessary changes so that your statement is personal, honest, and meaningful, and accurately describes you as an early childhood practitioner.

Figures 5-2 and 5-3 are exemplary philosophy statements written by college students in their early stages of developing a philosophy of education. Figures 5-4 and 5-5 are model philosophy statements from showcase portfolios. Notice that each philosophy statement expresses the views of that particular individual.

PHILOSOPHY OF EDUCATION

I believe that . . .

Each child is a gift.

Fun equates to engaging in active learning.

My job has great significance.

Each child is significant and has special needs.

A teacher is a facilitator of education.

Teaching will not only benefit the children, but also myself.

Children learn by interaction and play.

Communication between facilitator and parents is very important.

I can touch and have an impact on children's lives.

I will be a great teacher because it is such a huge part of who I am

And who I want to be.

FIGURE 5-2 *Early Philosophy of Education Statement*

My Philosophy of Education Statement

I believe that the goal of education is assisting children in discovering the different aspects of life. I believe it is important to give all children the opportunity and time to develop their minds at their own pace, but at the same time challenge them to think on their own rather than just listening to the educators' knowledge.

I believe that knowledge is gained through experiences. A child needs more than someone standing in front of them telling them what is right and wrong. Children need to see and experience different concepts to let them come to an understanding on their own. Knowledge cannot be forced on them, but directed to what amuses their minds.

I believe that the role of a teacher is to know each of her students and the way that learning comes naturally for them. A teacher should offer different aspects of teaching, allowing students to understand fully. Educators should allow children to feel comfortable and have complete trust in showing and sharing their weaknesses and problems. A teacher should not only be there for educational support, but also for emotional support. A teacher should let children know that if there are any problems, whether in or outside the classroom, the teacher is always there for guidance.

I believe that all children should have the opportunity to a full education. Children are born learners and are seeking someone to show them the world. In fact, children are our future. Children are not only learning from the teacher, the teacher is also learning from her own students. All children should know that one is never too big to ask questions and one never knows too much to learn something new.

I believe that a teacher should build and keep strong working relationships with parents and colleagues. A teacher should allow parents to know and be involved in what is going one in and outside the classroom. Teacher and parents should have a strong communication relationship in regard to their children's education and health. A teacher should reflect with colleagues to share ideas and experiences within the classroom, so that all can learn from each other.

FIGURE 5-3   *Early Philosophy of Education Statement*

Defining my personal philosophy of education is truly a daunting task. There are so many things I've learned and so much I want to incorporate that I could easily fill an entire book. Therefore, to keep this brief, I have selected a few quotes that I find reflect at least some of what I believe is important in the education of young children.

"Students learn what they care about . . .," Stanford Ericksen has said, but Goethe knew something else: "In all things we learn only from those we love." Add to that Emerson's declaration: "The secret of education lies in respecting the pupil," and we have a formula something like this: "Students learn what they care about, from people they care about and who, they know, care about them . . ."

—Barbara Harrell Carson, 1996, *Thirty Years of Stories*

It is vital that children feel loved, accepted, valued, and respected. Young children are open-hearted; they will respond to those who love them. It is also important for children to feel that what they are learning and doing in the classroom is valuable and interesting, not just beneficial.

"Tell me and I forget. Show me and I remember. Involve me and I understand."

—Chinese proverb

"A mind is a fire to be kindled, not a vessel to be filled."

—Plutarch

"If children are excited, curious, resourceful, and confident about their ability to figure things out and eager to exchange opinions with other adults and children, they are bound to go on learning, particularly when they are out of the classroom and throughout the rest of their lives."

—Constance Kamii

I see my role in the educational process as pivotal. It is up to every teacher to kindle the love of leaning, excitement, curiosity, and confidence in all of the children entrusted to his or her care. In all activities, the teacher serves as a model who can foster lifelong learning, respect, self-awareness, self-esteem, patience, and kindness; we can nurture all manner of high ideas, or not.

FIGURE 5-4 *Showcase Portfolio Philosophy of Education Statement*

Philosophy of Education Statement

"Too often we give our children answers to remember rather than problems to solve."
—Roger Lewin

This quote describes a large part of my educational philosophy, because it emphasizes that process is more important than content in the education of children. Content is the information that children learn, such as math facts, letters, words. Process is the ability to be able to problem-solve and think critically. It is the process by which children come to an answer that is more important than the answer itself. Children need to learn how to problem-solve and think critically much more than they need to memorize facts. Children who learn how to tackle a problem and think critically about a situation will be able to use these skills for their entire lives. Later in life, children will be presented with many problems to solve, whether in their careers or their daily lives. Children might benefit from memorizing their multiplication facts, and this memorization will indeed be useful later in life, but the more critical thing is to teach children how to work out multiplication problems for themselves. If children are taught why 2 times 2 equals 4 through the use of manipulative blocks and hands-on materials, they will understand multiplication. However, if children are taught to memorize 2 times 2 without understanding why this is, they will not understand multiplication and will not be able to solve new problems when they arise.

"Intelligence plus character—that is the goal of true education."
—Martin Luther King, Jr.

This is another quote that is a major part of my philosophy of education. I believe that is essential for children to learn about good character as well as to learn academics. I know that, in many schools, character education is a major part of the curriculum. Children are taught respect, caring, trustworthiness, responsibility, fairness, and citizenship. I believe that learning these pillars of good character is important. Children who can learn to be responsible will learn to turn assignments in on time and take responsibility for their own futures. Children who are taught respect will learn to have good relations with other people. Children who are taught to be trustworthy will be relied on and trusted. Having a good character is an essential part of being successful in a future career. Employers and college professors need to know that they can rely on their employees and students. I plan to incorporate character education in my future classrooms in many ways. I will post the six pillars of good character on the wall, so that my students can be reminded of them throughout the day. I will also praise and recognize students who show good character in their lives.

FIGURE 5-5　*Showcase Portfolio Philosophy of Education Statement*

ACTIVITY 5-1

Reading the four philosophy statements in Figures 5-2 through 5-5 should get your creative juices flowing. Try writing a philosophy statement that sums up your beliefs about children, families, teaching, and learning. How do you view yourself as an early childhood professional?

Begin by writing three words that describe yourself as a teacher.

1. _____

2. _____

3. _____

Write three beliefs you have about teaching.

1. _____

2. _____

3. _____

Identify three attributes of a good teacher

1. _____

2. _____

3. _____

Summary

Understanding that your philosophy statement is a work in progress is important, and we recommend that your philosophy statement be updated yearly. By examining your personal beliefs, your ideas about schools and schooling, and your understandings about people who are like you and different from you, you tell the readers what you want them to know about you. Writing your statement provides an opportunity for personal growth and satisfaction. It is critical that the writing be reflective, personal, and clear, and that your final document be well-organized and error-free so that it gives reviewers a vivid picture of you as a professional early childhood educator.

 ## Suggested Websites

If you need additional ideas, the Internet is full of examples of various types of philosophy statements. We found samples that were written in various styles at:

www.oregonstate.edu/instruct/ed416/sample.html

www.schoolmarm.org/portfolio/gen-phil.htm

www.uwrf.edu/ccs

www.reach.ucf.edu/~ed_found/gpi.html

www.qesnrecit.qc.ca/portfolio/eng/theory-R.html

www.ricteorg/T01_Library/T01_140.pdf

www.wilderdom.com/philosophy/SampleEducationPhilosophies.htm

http://Resumes-For-Teachers.com

http://ftad.osu.edu/portfolio/philosophy/Philosophy

www.ncrel.org/sdrs/areas/issues/students/earlycld/ea7lk18.htm

http://psychology.about.com/od/developmental psychology/a/childdevtheory.htm

 ## References

Berk, L. E. (2006). *Child development* (8th ed.). Boston, MA: Allyn & Bacon.

Crain, W. (2000). *Theories of development: Concepts and application* (6th ed.). Upper Saddle River, NJ: Prentice Hall.

Puckett, M. B., & Black, J. K. (2005). *The young child: Development from prebirth through age Eight* (5th ed.). Upper Saddle River, NJ: Pearson Merrill Prentice Hall.

Roopnarine, J. L., & Johnson, J. (2005). *Approaches to early childhood education* (4th ed.). Upper Saddle River, NJ: Merrill Prentice Hall.

chapter 6

· ·

Identifying Artifacts

An artifact is an object produced by humans. It can be a tool, a weapon, or an object of archaeological or historical interest; it can also be a mass-produced object that reflects the popular culture or contemporary society. The items or artifacts that you choose for your portfolio are exhibits that showcase what you know about teaching and learning. They are the pieces of evidence that make up your portfolio; they are shaped by you so that your portfolio documents and assesses your skills, and helps others understand you as an emerging early childhood professional. You may include any items that help you illustrate your abilities in meeting the portfolio criteria established by your school. While you are in the collecting and developmental stages, we recommend that you save a variety of artifacts, even if they are not necessarily representative of your "best" work. While "best work" portfolios are preferred by some, others see a value in selecting some work that may not exemplify best practices. For example, perhaps you tried a lesson that was unsuccessful. Did you learn from this experience? Of course you did. So you might want to include one not-so-successful lesson to explain what you would do differently if you were to try that lesson again. Artifacts should provide an authentic picture of your strengths and areas of need. They allow you to set goals for self-improvement. Some authorities on portfolios suggest that even the final showcase portfolio include evidence of both strengths and weaknesses (Burke, 1999); however, most feel that your interview portfolio should represent only your best work (Antonek, McCormick, & Donato, 1997; Constantino & DeLorenzo, 2009).

Artifacts describe what you know and what you can do (Jones & Shelton, 2006). You can include paper documents, electronic documents, electronic images, photographs, and audio- and videotapes. Potential artifacts that can go in Section II of your portfolio are listed in Figure 6-1. Artifacts from early childhood courses are listed in Figure 6-2, and artifacts appropriate for each of the NAEYC Standards are listed in Figure 6-3. This should give you many ideas for possible artifacts and how to use them with the standards.

Artifact	Completed/Provided
Action research project	
Activity ideas	
Adaptations of materials or instruction	
Annotated Book List	
Article critiques/reviews	
Arts integration	
Assessments (formal, informal, summative, formative)	
Assessment strategies	
Audiotapes	
Bulletin board creations	
Case studies/Child studies	
Checklists, rubrics developed	
Classroom designs	
Classroom management plans and projects	
Community service projects	
Diagnostic reports	
Diversity ideas	
Evaluations or lists of developmentally appropriate software	
Exhibits	
Family or parental projects	
Field trip plans and experiences	
Flannel board ideas	
Interactions with children, demonstrated on video	
Instructional strategies, materials, designs, activities	
Interviews with parents, teachers, specialists, administrators, children	
Journal entries	
Learning centers	
Lesson plans	
Letters to colleagues, community workers, parents	
List of resources and services for students and teachers	
Literature for children	
Logs	
Meetings	
Music ideas and activities	

FIGURE 6-1 *Potential Artifacts for Section II of Your Portfolio*
This is not a complete list of artifacts. Preservice teachers will have many and varied experiences and can provide artifacts that have affected their learning.

Artifact	Completed/Provided
Newsletters	
Observation reports	
Observation tools	
Reactions to newspaper articles/reports	
Personal/professional assessment	
Philosophy statement	
Photographs	
Play: value, ideas, and integration	
Posters created	
PowerPoint presentations	
Presentations	
Professional development	
Professional literature	
Puppets	
Prop boxes	
References	
Reflections	
Research papers and reports	
Resource files and lists	
Rubrics	
Self-evaluations, assessments and teacher evaluations	
Service learning projects	
Simulations	
Student work samples	
Technology use in the classroom	
Technology review/competencies	
Testimonies	
Thematic units	
Transition ideas	
Units of instruction	
Videotape critiques	
Volunteer work and experiences	
Websites	
Written test	

FIGURE 6-1 *Potential Artifacts for Section II of Your Portfolio (continued)*

Course Description	Sample Artifacts that Might be Appropriate for Your Portfolio
Introduction to early childhood education (any beginning level course where portfolio is introduced).	Autobiographical paper Theorist research paper Paper on problems and trends in Early childhood education Article reflections or critiques Observation in early childhood settings Philosophy statement Newsletter to parents or families
Any child development course.	Case studies Article reflections or critiques Report on stages of development (infant, toddler, pre-K, kindergarten, Grades 1, 2, and 3) Report or paper on types of development (social, emotional, cognitive, physical, literacy) Paper or presentation on developmental theorists (Piaget, Vygotsky, Erikson, Freud, Gesell, Gardner, Maslow, and others) Paper on atypical development
Introduction to special education course.	Report on an individual education plan (IEP) meeting Paper on the characteristics of exceptionalities Observation in an inclusive environment Adaptive strategies report or demonstration Paper that documents understanding of the laws and litigation
Any course geared to infant development.	Field observations in an infant center Field observations in a shelter Community service project in a shelter Parenting newsletter Report on Head Start Investigative piece on services and resources for families
Any course that addresses teaching in a multicultural, multi-ethnic society.	Interview with someone from a culture different from your own An object that reflects your own culture Community service project A list of stereotypical items found in a classroom
Any course that addresses issues of interactive technology and early childhood education.	Early childhood software review/critique Observations of children using technology Review and analysis of websites appropriate for young children A PowerPoint presentation in the classroom Electronic portfolios Using technology to enhance your resume Multimedia presentation
Reading course aimed at studying theories, processes, and acquisition of reading and language arts, including cognitive, linguistic, social, and physiological factors involved in oral and written language development.	Research project on reading/writing Literacy acquisition study Memory retrieval test Issues in literacy paper Writing sample analysis Article critique on phonics Presentation/paper on theorists in the field of reading/language arts

FIGURE 6-2   *Sample Artifacts from Early Childhood Courses*

Course Description	Sample Artifacts that Might be Appropriate for Your Portfolio
A course on advanced writing for early childhood majors.	Resume Parent newsletter Letter of recommendation for a student A letter of referral Reflective journal writings
Preprimary curriculum course that involves best practices in curriculum and methods of teaching children between 4 and 6 years of age.	Ethic/moral dilemma paper using NAEYC code of ethics Letter of introduction to field placement mentor-teacher Reflective journal writing Attendance/report on a nonteaching school event Lesson plans Center activity plan Dramatic play prop box Integrated web Integrated unit Project involving families Revise philosophy statement
Emergent literacy course examines strategies, materials, and experiences for literacy development in children from birth to age 5.	Word story activity to be taught and critiqued Lesson plans in phonemic awareness, phonics, vocabulary development, comprehension, and fluency Family literacy bag Shared reading lesson Phonemic awareness lesson A lesson involving rhyming words Read-aloud lesson Design a literacy center Evaluation of pre-K and kindergarten literacy programs
One course or multiple courses that address the teaching and integration of the arts (music, drama, dance, movement, drawing) for young children.	Lesson plan using the arts to teach a prereading activity Design centers incorporating the arts Teach and reflect on a movement activity done in your placement Draw-a-story activity
Any course in science methods that familiarizes students with appropriate content, methods, materials, and evaluation of teaching science to the young child.	A case study documenting science learning in the classroom Plan and execute a lesson that analyzes data, forms generalizations about the data, and applies the explanation to another situation or problem. Design a hands-on science center Design a science lesson that integrates another content area
Mathematics methods in early childhood education.	Design a math game Plan, execute, and assess a math lesson in your placement Create a chart or graph that illustrates and organizes data
Methods for identifying and assessing disabilities in early childhood education.	Attend an IEP meeting Use the Developmental Activities Screening Inventory (DASI) to assess a child Write a recommendation to parents for intervention strategies for a child identified with a disability Paper on a specific disability

FIGURE 6-2   *Sample Artifacts from Early Childhood Courses (continued)*

Course Description	Sample Artifacts that Might be Appropriate for Your Portfolio
A course that examines and uses a range of literacy and reading assessments and that focuses on the relationship of assessment to instructional planning for diverse learners.	Use miscue analysis on a child to detect reading strengths and weaknesses Reading and writing sample analysis Analyze the results for the Motivation to Read survey Running records
A course on teaching reading in the primary grades (1 to 3), with emphasis on best practices, research, materials, and developmentally appropriate active learning related to the process of learning to read.	Child literacy study Plan, execute, and assess a directed reading lesson Plan, execute, and assess a guided reading lesson Plan, execute, and assess a fluency, vocabulary, phonics, or phonemic awareness lesson Running records to evaluate a child's reading Behavior management plan
One or more methods courses that look at developmentally appropriate objectives, materials, lesson plans, activities, methods, and assessments for teaching all content areas (science, social studies, language arts, mathematics) in grades 1 to 3.	Plan, execute, and assess one lesson in every content area Field trip plan Videotape and critical reflection of your teaching Peer observation/critique Service learning project Classroom management plan Cycle of learning (two, three, or five concurrent lessons using pre- and postassessments) Journal reflections Interview your mentor-teacher about the profession
The final student teaching experience involving 16 weeks in a public school.	Write daily lesson plans Evaluations and assessment of students (informal, formal) Attend IEP meetings Three-day cycle of learning plan with reflection Unit plans Design and use a classroom management plan Daily reflection log Design and execute a bulletin board Reflect on differentiation in your classroom Revise philosophy statement
Other	

FIGURE 6-2 *Sample Artifacts from Early Childhood Courses (continued)*

Choosing Appropriate Artifacts

How you select artifacts for your portfolio depends on your stage of development and the purpose of your portfolio. If you are in the collection and development stages, collect a wide range of many and diverse artifacts. When you are refining materials for a showcase or interview portfolio, your task changes. In the beginning, you are selecting the best evidence to represent your competencies in the many

NAEYC Standards	Suggested Artifacts that Might be Appropriate Under Each Standard
1. Promoting Child Development and Learning 1a: Knowing and understanding young children's characteristics and needs. 1b: Knowing and understanding the multiple influences on development and learning. 1c: Using developmental knowledge to create healthy, respectful, supportive, and challenging learning environments.	Observations of various early childhood settings. Case studies. Report or research on the stages of development. Report of research on the developmental theorists (Piaget, Vygotsky, Erikson, Freud, Gessell, Gardner, Maslow, and others). Observation of an atypically developing child. A paper on exceptionalities. Observation in an inclusive environment. Report on strategies in an early childhood classroom. Review of early childhood software. Observation of children using technology. A literacy acquisition study. Student writing samples. Written and enacted lesson plans. A dramatic play box. Evaluation of a pre-K or kindergarten literacy program. Learning centers. Developmental screening tools to assess a child.
2. Building Family and Community Relationships 2a: Knowing about and understanding diverse family and community characteristics. 2b: Supporting and engaging families and communities through respectful, reciprocal relationships. 2c: Involving families and communities in their children's development and learning.	A philosophy statement. A newsletter to parents. Report on an individual education plan (IEP) meeting. A paper on laws and litigation involving children, families, and schools. Interview of someone from a culture other than your own. Investigation of services and resources to support families at your field placement school. A community service project. A family literacy bag. Reflection on parent-teacher conferences. Notes from a parent workshop or a PTA meeting. An ethical dilemma paper. A project involving families. An object that reflects your own culture.
3. Observing, Documenting, and Assessing to support Young Children and Families 3a: Understanding the goals, benefits, and uses of assessment. 3b: Knowing about assessment partnerships with families and with professional colleagues. 3c: Knowing about and using observation, documentation, and other appropriate assessment tools and approaches.	Observation of pre-K, kindergarten, or grades 1, 2, and 3. Observation of children with special needs. Observation of an experienced teacher. A case study. Report or critique of an article from a professional journal. Report of research stages of development. Research or observation of typical and atypical development. Observation in inclusive settings. Research of characteristics of exceptionalities. Report on adaptive strategies. Field observations in an infant center, shelter, or other school setting.

FIGURE 6-3 *Sample Artifacts under NAEYC Standards for Early Childhood Professional Preparation Programs*

NAEYC Standards	Suggested Artifacts that Might be Appropriate Under Each Standard
	Evaluation of pre-K and kindergarten literacy programs. A learning center. Developmental screening tools to assess a child. A project involving families. Revision of your philosophy statement. A family literacy bag. Reflections on an IEP meeting. A service learning project. Notes on parent workshops. Lesson plans that include assessments and reflection. Reading assessments (running records, miscue analysis, IRI). A child literacy study. Videotape and critique of your own teaching. Formal and informal assessments. Application of differentiation in your classroom. Execution of a three-day cycle of learning.
4. Using Developmentally Effective approaches to Connect with Children and Families 4a: Understanding positive relationships and supportive interactions as the foundation of their work with children. 4b: Knowing and understanding effective strategies and tools for early education. 4c: Using a broad repertoire of developmentally appropriate teaching/learning approaches. 4d: Reflecting on their own practice to promote positive outcomes for each child.	Observation in an inclusive environment. Classroom management plan. Report on adaptive strategies. Review of early childhood software. Observation of children using technology. Lesson plan using technology in the classroom. Evaluation of a pre-K or Kindergarten literacy program. A learning center. A service learning project. An action research project. Notes on an IEP meeting. Developmental screening tools to assess a child. Notes on parent workshops or PTA meetings. Attendance at a parent-teacher conference. Reflections on the use of different approaches to teaching. Regular journal reflections.
5. Using Content Knowledge to Build Meaningful Curriculum 5a: Understanding content knowledge and resources in academic disciplines. 5b: Knowing and using the central concepts, inquiry tools, and structures of content areas or academic disciplines. 5c: Using their own knowledge, appropriate early learning standards, and other resources to design, implement, and evaluate meaningful, challenging curricula for each child.	Theorist research paper. A center activity. Reflections on teaching a small-group lesson. An integrated unit. Student writing samples. Execution of a three- or five-day cycle of learning. Use and implementation of various assessments. A dramatic play box. Lesson plans that utilize computer skills to enhance learning. Detailed lesson plans based on national/state standards. A classroom management plan. A case study to document learning. Research on services and resources to support families. Evaluation of curriculum materials. Regular journal reflections.

FIGURE 6-3 *Sample Artifacts under NAEYC Standards for Early Childhood Professional Preparation Programs (continued)*

NAEYC Standards	Suggested Artifacts that Might be Appropriate Under Each Standard
	A recommendation to parents for intervention strategies for a child identified with a disability. Meaningful lesson plans in all content areas. Lesson plans that integrate the arts into the curriculum.
6. Becoming a Professional 6a: Identifying and involving oneself with the early childhood field. 6b: Knowing about and upholding ethical standards and other professional guidelines. 6c: Engaging in continuous, collaborative learning to inform practice. 6d: Integrating knowledgeable, reflective, and critical perspectives on early education. 6e: Engaging in informed advocacy for children and the profession.	Revision of your philosophy statement. An autobiographical paper. Interviews of teachers, school faculty, parents or children. Case studies. Activities that advocate for young children. Notes on professional meetings or conferences. Regular reflective journals. Notes and reflections on team meetings. A resume. A letter of referral. A daily reflection log in your placement.

FIGURE 6-3 *Sample Artifacts under NAEYC Standards for Early Childhood Professional Preparation Programs (continued)*

areas being assessed. Answering the questions posed by Constantino and DeLorenzo (2009, p. 49) will help you determine whether the document is worthy of inclusion. It is important to remember that building your portfolio is an ongoing process, and you may choose to include or discard artifacts throughout the various phases of development. As you choose artifacts, it is important to continually ask yourself the following questions:

- Does the evidence provided align with the purpose of my portfolio?
- Does the evidence support the standard or theme (NAEYC/InTASC)?
- Is the evidence provided credible and does it support progress toward my professional growth, learning, and goals?
- Does the evidence provide substance and meaning to my portfolio?
- Could the evidence detract from the credibility of my portfolio?

Which Artifacts Are Best for My Portfolio?

The NAEYC standards, InTASC standards, or other standards are used as criteria; they form the framework for portfolio development in early childhood education. Of course, only you can decide which artifacts are best for your portfolio. Suggestions from your professors, instructors, and peers are often helpful. However, selection of items depends on the purpose and the type of portfolio. You want to meet the indicators for each standard fully. We are using NAEYC standards for the dividers of evidence in the professional background section of your portfolio, and as you have already seen, Figure 6-3 provides artifacts using those standards.

Start collecting artifacts for your portfolio today! The NAEYC and InTASC standards, or other standards used as criteria are the framework for portfolio development in early childhood education; start selecting artifacts that represent them. One way to do this is by charting collected evidence on a grid. Figure 6-4 is a grid for charting the evidence you have collected using the NAEYC Standards. Figure 6-5 is a grid for using both NAEYC and InTASC standards. It also includes InTASC performance, essential knowledge, and critical disposition indicators to use as a specific element under each standard. It is recommended that you also create a folder (manila or computer) and collect your artifacts in it. As you go, add each artifact to a list. Add a simple descriptive statement, such as "Child literacy study," to help you see how the artifact fits into your portfolio. You could also identify the artifact and the specific standard that it represents, such as "Child literacy study—NAEYC 3a."

NAEYC Standards	Evidence I Have	Evidence I Hope to Obtain
1. Promoting Child Development and Learning 1a: Knowing and understanding young children's characteristics and needs. 1b: Knowing and understanding the multiple influences on development and learning. 1c: Using developmental knowledge to create healthy, respectful, supportive, and challenging learning environments.		
2. Building Family and Community Relationships 2a: Knowing about and understanding diverse family and community characteristics. 2b: Supporting and engaging families and communities through respectful, reciprocal relationships. 2c: Involving families and communities in their children's development and learning.		
3. Observing, Documenting, and Assessing to support Young Children and Families 3a: Understanding the goals, benefits, and uses of assessment. 3b: Knowing about assessment partnerships with families and with professional colleagues. 3c: Knowing about and using observation, documentation, and other appropriate assessment tools and approaches.		

FIGURE 6-4   *Grid for Charting Collected Evidence Using NAEYC Standards for Early Childhood Professional Preparation Programs*

NAEYC Standards	Evidence I Have	Evidence I Hope to Obtain
4. Using Developmentally Effective approaches to Connect with Children and Families 4a: Understanding positive relationships and supportive interactions as the foundation of their work with children. 4b: Knowing and understanding effective strategies and tools for early education. 4c: Using a broad repertoire of developmentally appropriate teaching/learning approaches. 4d: Reflecting on their own practice to promote positive outcomes for each child.		
5. Using Content Knowledge to Build Meaningful Curriculum 5a: Understanding content knowledge and resources in academic disciplines. 5b: Knowing and using the central concepts, inquiry tools, and structures of content areas or academic disciplines. 5c: Using their own knowledge, appropriate early learning standards, and other resources to design, implement, and evaluate meaningful, challenging curricula for each child.		
6. Becoming a Professional 6a: Identifying and involving oneself with the early childhood field. 6b: Knowing about and upholding ethical standards and other professional guidelines. 6c: Engaging in continuous, collaborative learning to inform practice. 6d: Integrating knowledgeable, reflective, and critical perspectives on early education. 6e: Engaging in informed advocacy for children and the profession.		

FIGURE 6-4 *Grid for Charting Collected Evidence Using NAEYC Standards for Early Childhood Professional Preparation Programs (continued)*

NAEYC Standards for Early Childhood Professional Preparation Programs	InTASC Model Core Teaching Standard	InTASC Performance Indicators	InTASC Essential Knowledge Indicators	InTASC Critical Disposition Indicators	Evidence I Have Collected	Evidence I Need to Collect
1. Promoting Child Development and Learning	1. Learner Development	1 (a–c)	1 (d–g)	1 (h–k)		
2. Building Family and Community Relationships	1. Learner Development	1 (c)		1 (k)		
	2. Learning Differences	2 (d)	2 (l, k)	2 (m)		
	3. Learning Environments	3 (a, c, e, f)		3 (n)		
	5. Innovative Applications of Content			5 (n)		
	6. Assessment					
	7. Planning for Instruction			7 (o)		
	8. Instructional Strategies	8 (c, h, i)	8 (q)	8 (m)		
	9. Reflection and Continuous Growth	9 (b)		9 (m)		
	10. Collaboration	10 (c–e, g, k)	10 (m)	10 (n, q)		
3. Observing, Documenting, and Assessing to Support Young Children and Families	1. Learner Development	1 (a, b)	1 (d–g)	1 (h, i, k)		
	2. Learning Differences	2 (a–f), 2 (h)	2 (g, h, j, k)	2 (l, m, n, o)		
	3. Learning Environments	3 (d, f)	3 (l)			
	4. Content Knowledge	4 (a, d–g)	4 (l, m)	4 (r)		
	6. Assessment	6 (a–i)	6 (j–p)	6 (q–v)		
	7. Planning for Instruction	7 (b, c, d, f)	7 (i–m)	7 (n, q)		
	8. Instructional Strategies	8 (a, b, d–f)	8 (k)	8 (p, s)		
	9. Professional Learning and Ethical Practice	9 (a, c, e)	9 (g–j)	9 (m)		
	10. Collaboration	10 (a, b)				

FIGURE 6-5 *Grid for Charting Collected Evidence Using NAEYC and InTASC Standards*

NAEYC Standards for Early Childhood Professional Preparation Programs	InTASC Model Core Teaching Standard	InTASC Performance Indicators	InTASC Essential Knowledge Indicators	InTASC Critical Disposition Indicators	Evidence I Have Collected	Evidence I Need to Collect
4. Using Developmentally Effective Approaches to Connect with Children and Families	1. Learner Development	1 (a, b)	1 (d–g)	1 (h, i, k)		
	2. Learning Differences	2 (a–f), 2 (h)	2 (g, h, j, k)	2 (l–o)		
	3. Learning Environments	3 (d, f, g, h)	3 (l)	3 (j, m)		
	4. Content Knowledge	4 (a, d, e–g)	4 (l, m)	4 (r)		
	5. Innovative Applications of Content	5 (c)		5 (k, l)		
	6. Assessment	6 (a–i)	6 (j–p)	6 (q–v)		
	7. Planning for Instruction	7 (b, c, d, f)	7 (i–m)	7 (k, n, q)		
	8. Instructional Strategies	8 (a, b, d–g)	8 (k, q, r)	8 (n–p, s)		
	9. Reflection and Continuous Growth	9 (a, e, f)	9 (g–j)	9 (m)		
	10. Collaboration	10 (e, g)		10 (n)		
5. Using Content Knowledge to Build Meaningful Curriculum	4. Content Knowledge	4 (a–i)	4 (j–n)	4 (o–r)		
	5. Innovative Applications of Content	5 (a–h)	T (i–p)	5 (q–s)		
	6. Assessment	7 (a–f)	7 (g–m)	7 (n–q)		
	7. Planning for Instruction	8 (a–i)	8 (j–o)	8 (p–s)		
6. Becoming a Professional	4. Content Knowledge			4 (o, p, q)		
	5. Innovative Applications of Content			5 (q, r)		
	6. Assessment	6 (a, c, g, i)	6 (j–p)	6 (t)		
	7. Planning for Instruction		7 (f, k)			
	8. Instructional Strategies	8 (g)	8 (k, n, o)	8 (p)		
	9. Reflection and Continuous Growth	9 (a–f)	9 (g–k)	9 (l–o)		
	10. Collaboration	10 (a–k)	10 (l–o)	10 (p–t)		

FIGURE 6-5 *Grid for Charting Collected Evidence Using NAEYC and InTASC Standards (continued)*

Portfolio Evidence(Artifact)	Possible NAEYC Standard(s) and Substandard(s)	Possible InTASC Standard(s) and Substandard(s)
Toddler case study	1 (a)	1 (d–f), 7 (f)
English for speakers of other languages (ESOL) parent interview	2 (a–c)	2 (d, f, k, m, o, q), 9 (g, k)
Reading assessment (running record, IRI, or miscue analysis)	3 (c)	6 (e, h, i, m, p)
Behavior management plan	4 (a–c)	3 (a, c, d, f, k), 5 (b, c, p, s)
Planning and execution of a cycle of learning	5 (a–c)	3 (a, c, d, f, i, j, m), 4 (a–d, f, k, m), 5 (a, c, m, n, p, v, w), 7 (a–d, 7e g, i, j), 8 (b, g, h, j), 9 (h)
Presentation of an action research project at a professional conference	6 (a, c, d)	9 (n), 10 (d)
Your Artifact	**NAEYC Standard(s) and Substandard(s)**	**InTASC Standard(s) and Substandard(s)**
	NAEYC Standard 1	
	NAEYC Standard 2	
	NAEYC Standard 3	
	NAEYC Standard 4	
	NAEYC Standard 5	

FIGURE 6-6   NAEYC and InTASC Standards Cross-Reference Guide

ACTIVITY 6-1

Look at the lists of possible artifacts that have been suggested in this chapter. Using any of them and a system that works best for you, devise your own list of artifacts that you have collected. Use the sample charts provided in Figure 6-3, Figure 6-4, or Figure 6-5 to check off artifacts you have already collected. Remember that you should vary your artifacts so that you show all aspects of your scholarship, teaching, and experiences with young children. Using a checklist or other type of notation system allows you to keep track of the artifacts that you have selected for use in your portfolio.

ACTIVITY 6-2

Using Figure 6-6 as a cross-reference guide, identify one artifact from each of the NAEYC standards and correlate it with an InTASC standard and substandard. One example from each NAEYC standard is presented to help you get started.

Summary

In this chapter, we have explained what artifacts are and how to choose them for your portfolio. Artifacts are tangible evidence of your developing skills in the field of early childhood education. They should demonstrate your knowledge, skills, and dispositions as a young teacher. Artifacts can come from your professional early childhood courses and from your many field experiences as a preservice teacher. Choosing artifacts is a highly personal endeavor and depends on your stage of development. The artifacts that you select now should not be considered permanent. They should change over time to reflect your continual growth as a professional.

 # Suggested Websites

General artifacts for K–12 teachers:

http://midsolutions.org/prtfolios/general/htm

The Role of Critical Reflection in the Portfolio Process. Online professional development from Johns Hopkins University and Morgan State University.

www.sitesupport.org/module1/portfolio.htm

What is reflection? Online from UW-Whitewater.

www.uwstout.edu/careers/portfolios.shtml

Sample portfolio artifacts for the teacher education working portfolio

www.regis.edu/content/cpedcn/pdf/apg.gp.med. pp.COPortfolioSample.pdf

 # References

Anatonek, J. L., McCormick, D. E., & Donato, R. (1997). The student teacher portfolio as autobiography: Developing a professional identity. *Modern Language Journal, 81,* 5–27.

Burke, K. (1999). *How to assess authentic learning* (3rd ed.). Arlington Heights, IL: Skylight Training.

Costantino, P. M., & DeLorenzo, M. N. (2009). *Developing a professional teaching portfolio: A guide for success* (3rd ed.). New York: Pearson.

Jones, M., & Shelton, M. (2006). *Developing your portfolio: Enhancing your learning and showing your stuff: A guide for the early childhood student or professional.* New York: Routledge.

chapter 7

. . . .

Writing Your Reflective Narrative

Reflection, the act of being contemplative, thoughtful, or meditative, is the defining characteristic of the portfolio. Through reflection, you show your thinking about the six major standards from the National Association for the Education of Young Children (NAEYC): promoting child development and learning; building family and community relationships; observing, documenting, and assessing to support young children and families; using developmentally effective approaches to connect with children and families; using content knowledge to build meaningful curriculum; and becoming a professional (NAEYC Standards for Early Childhood Professional Preparation Programs, 2009). Reflection shows where your practice and pedagogy merge. The process of reflecting enhances self-evaluation of your teaching and learning, bringing together your prior knowledge and fresh new awareness.

What Is a Reflective Narrative?

A reflective narrative is aimed to reflect on a specific personal event or experience. Your perceptions of that event reveal your understanding of the episode. Artifacts used as evidence of NAEYC or InTASC standards must be accompanied by a reflective narrative that explains why the evidence or document was chosen to be included in the portfolio and why it serves as evidence for the standards. However, you may use your own creativity, the ability to change a standard perception to a unique one, and your attitude about the social phenomenon to vary your writing. For example, the book bag comprehension lesson in Figure 7-1 addresses NAEYC Standard 5a and InTASC Standard 7b. Notice how the student provides evidence of why her lesson meets the standards she designates, and how the lesson exemplifies her own creativity in lesson planning, execution, and assessment procedures.

Book Bag Comprehension Lesson

NAEYC Standard 5: Using Content Knowledge to Build Meaningful Curriculum (a) Understanding content knowledge and resources in academic disciplines.

InTASC Principle 7: Planning for Instruction (b)The teacher plans how to achieve student learning goals, choosing appropriate strategies, resources, and materials to differentiate instruction for individuals and groups of students; developing appropriate sequencing of learning experiences; and allowing multiple ways to demonstrate knowledge and skill.

For my foundations of language arts course, I composed a book bag for the picture book *Scaredy Mouse* and wrote a lesson plan that required the use of the book bag to enhance comprehension skills. The use of the book bag demonstrated my ability to use one of the wide variety of resources available to enhance student learning. Because the highly motivating book bag engaged students in the lesson, I was able to achieve my comprehension objectives. Students used the book bag materials to be actively involved while I read the story. The active engagement that this book bag elicited ameliorated some of the limitations of whole-group instruction. Following the reading, students used the book bag props to sequence the story events. My use of props for sequencing demonstrated my understanding of the cognitive processes associated with comprehension. Students were more likely to recall important information when they had tactile and visual models of the event. My assessment for this book used a unique flip book that I designed to match the text. By using a creative assessment tool rather than a standard worksheet, the students demonstrated strong performance skills in their responses.

This lesson aligns with NAEYC Standard 5a and InTASC Standard 7b because I used high-quality resources to enhance students' thinking skills. My knowledge of the content area allowed me to plan a reading approach that would engage all students. I developed appropriate sequencing activities, included many open-ended questions that assessed students' thinking skills, and provided multiple avenues for success. By completing this book bag, I learned how teachers can promote higher-level thinking skills using unique instructional strategies.

FIGURE 7-1 *A Lesson That Addresses NAEYC Standard 5a and InTASC Standard 7b*

What a Reflective Narrative Is Not

A reflective narrative is *not* a caption! A caption simply labels the artifact in one or two sentences. Captions are acceptable for items in the appendix to your portfolio, such as letters from parents and students, or photographs not specific to a lesson or activity, but not in the reflective narrative. Captions lack the reflective, personal perceptiveness; the reasons that a particular artifact fits into a certain standard; and what learning has transpired by the teacher and the students.

How Your Reflective Narrative Relates to Your Philosophy Statement

Your personal learning experiences, teaching style, and philosophy define who you are as a young professional. Your ideas and understandings about teaching and learning are a product of your prior educational experiences, life events, and the observations you have made about children's development in the classroom. As you learned earlier, your portfolio usually begins with your philosophy—a concise statement that combines educational theory and pedagogy with practice.

The artifacts in your portfolio, accompanied by a reflective narrative, should be an extension of your philosophy. Here, you have the opportunity to select artifacts for inclusion in your portfolio that will infuse your personal beliefs and values with your understanding of theory and practice. Instructional lesson plans presented alone in a portfolio are just that, instructional lesson plans. An artifact without any explanation of learning has no meaning to the reader or reviewer. The reflective narrative that accompanies an artifact is what separates a portfolio from a scrapbook or simply a collection of materials. Reflection is what shows your learning, growth, and understanding over time. Evidence of your thinking and deliberation is where beliefs and values meet education theory in your quest to become a reflective practitioner.

How Does the Artifact Connect to the NAEYC and InTASC Standards?

Connecting your artifact to the NAEYC standards takes thought and practice. If your school or institution uses a rubric for assessment, the indicators for meeting that standard may also help you better understand each standard and principle. Our university (Towson University) now uses the NAEYC standards as the main divisions under which artifacts are placed, but it also incorporates InTASC standards. For example, in Figure 7-2, the heading for the reflective narrative includes the title of the artifact, the date the artifact was collected, the course the intern was taking, and the numbers of the NAEYC and InTASC standards and their subheadings. The subheadings under each standard are denoted by the letter in the parentheses.

Our university also uses the same portfolio assessment forms (see Figures 7-3 and 7-4) throughout the portfolio development process, as well as for the final summative assessment. The consistency of using the same assessment measures again and again is valuable for students. The Portfolio Assessment Tool using NAEYC Standards (Figure 7-3) is divided into two sections. The first column is the NAEYC Core Standard and its key elements. The second column lists the indicators that are based on NAEYC and InTASC Standards. For example, under NAEYC Standard 1: Promoting Child Development and Learning, you might include a research paper you wrote on autism where you not only explained this disorder, but also showed how autistic children might differ

---

Read-Aloud

Spring 2011   ECED 360

NAEYC Standard 4: Using Developmentally Effective Approaches (d) Reflecting on their own practice to promote positive outcomes for each child.
InTASC Standard 3: Learning Environments. (b) The teacher collaborates with students to develop shared values and expectations for respectful interaction, thoughtful academic discussions, and individual and group responsibility that create a positive learning climate and openness, mutual respect, support, and inquiry.

FIGURE 7-2 *Sample Heading for Your Reflective Narrative*

from typically developing children. This would meet indicator 1 (shows knowledge of typical and atypical development). This same artifact would nicely fit under InTASC Standard 1 (Figure 7-4), Learner Development, and indicator 1 (shows knowledge of typical and atypical growth and development). Figure 7-3 uses NAEYC standards as the guiding standards, while Figure 7-4 uses the InTASC standards.

Both portfolio assessment tools are helpful in understanding what reviewers are looking for because all your artifacts should meet all indicators under each standard. Using some of the language of the standards and the indicators in your reflective narrative helps reviewers know that you have met that standard.

NAEYC Standard	Indicators
1. Promoting Child Development and Learning 1a: Knowing and understanding young children's characteristics and needs. 1b: Knowing and understanding the multiple influences on development and learning. 1c: Using developmental knowledge to create healthy, respectful, supportive, and challenging learning environments.	Shows knowledge of typical and atypical growth and development. Designs instruction that meets learner's current needs based on age, ability, development, learning style, readiness, culture, social group, and/or values. Understands learning theory, human development, cultural diversity, and individual differences.
2. Building Family and Community Relationships 2a: Knowing about and understanding diverse family and community characteristics. 2b: Supporting and engaging families and communities through respectful, reciprocal relationships. 2c: Involving families and communities in their children's development and learning.	Identifies and uses community resources to foster student learning and success. Communicates effectively with families, teachers, and resource personnel to foster student learning and success. Shows understanding of the alignment of family, school, and community.
3. Observing, Documenting, and Assessing to support Young Children and Families 3a: Understanding the goals, benefits, and uses of assessment. 3b: Knowing about assessment partnerships with families and with professional colleagues. 3c: Knowing about and using observation, documentation, and other appropriate assessment tools and approaches.	Uses multiple and appropriate types of assessments to identify needs, develop differentiated learning experiences, and document learning. Uses pre- and postassessments to diagnose, monitor, and document student progress. Uses information obtained from review of student work to plan and modify instruction. Designs formative assessments that match learning objectives to help learners demonstrate knowledge and skills.
4. Using Developmentally Effective Approaches to Connect with Children and Families 4a: Understanding positive relationships and supportive interactions as the foundation of their work with children. 4b: Knowing and understanding effective strategies and tools for early education. 4c: Using a broad repertoire of developmentally appropriate teaching/learning approaches. 4d: Reflecting on their own practice to promote positive outcomes for each child.	Supports and expands learners' communication through speaking, listening, reading, writing, and other media. Uses appropriate strategies and resources to adapt to the needs of individual students (e.g. prior knowledge, interests, developmental differences). Integrates technological tools to engage students, families, and/or colleagues. Respects families' norms and expectations and works collaboratively with students and families in meeting goals.

FIGURE 7-3 *Portfolio Assessment Tool Using NAEYC Standards*

NAEYC Standard	Indicators
5. Using Content Knowledge to Build Meaningful Curriculum 5a: Understanding content knowledge and resources in academic disciplines. 5b: Knowing and using the central concepts, inquiry tools, and structures of content areas or academic disciplines. 5c: Using their own knowledge, appropriate early learning standards, and other resources to design, implement, and evaluate meaningful, challenging curricula for each child.	Selects learning experiences that connect content to national/state/local standards and are relevant to learners. Focuses instruction on essential concepts, inquiry tools, and methods of inquiry in the discipline. Explores the use of new technologies that support and promote student learning. Designs, implements and evaluates differentiated instruction for a diverse and inclusive community of students.
6. Becoming a Professional 6a: Identifying and involving oneself with the early childhood field. 6b: Knowing about and upholding ethical standards and other professional guidelines. 6c: Engaging in continuous, collaborative learning to inform practice. 6d: Integrating knowledgeable, reflective, and critical perspectives on early education. 6e: Engaging in informed advocacy for children and the profession.	Integrates classroom observations and analyses of data about students to evaluate the outcomes of teaching and revise practice. Consults professional literature, colleagues, and other professional learning opportunities to advance your own and/or student learning. Engages in professional learning to enhance knowledge and skills. Engages in advocacy for children and the profession and models safe, legal, and ethical behavior. Participates actively as a part of an instructional team.

FIGURE 7-3 Portfolio Assessment Tool Using NAEYC Standards (continued)

Many universities endorsed by the National Council of Accreditation for Teacher Education (NCATE) still use the 10 InTASC standards as guides to show what early childhood educators should know and be able do in a classroom. Figure 7-4 illustrates a portfolio assessment tool using the new InTASC Model Core Teaching Standards (Council of Chief State School Officers, 2011). This tool is also divided into two sections. The first column is the InTASC standard; the right-hand second column lists the indicators for that standard. Note the similarities between the two portfolio assessment tools, which indicates a consistency in the two assessments.

InTASC Standard	Indicators
1. Learner Development The teacher understands how learners grow and develop, recognizing that patterns of learning and development vary individually within and across the cognitive, linguistic, social, emotional, and physical areas, and designs and implements developmentally appropriate and challenging learning experiences.	Shows knowledge of typical and atypical growth and development. Designs instruction that meets learner's current needs based on age, ability, development, learning style, readiness, culture, social group, and/or values. Understands learning theory, human development, cultural diversity, and individual differences.
2. Learning Differences The teacher uses understanding of individual differences and diverse cultures and communities to ensure inclusive learning environments that enable each learner to meet high standards.	Designs, adapts, and delivers instruction to address each student's diverse learning strengths and needs. Values diverse languages and dialects and seeks to integrate them into instructional practice.

FIGURE 7-4 Portfolio Assessment Tool Using InTASC Standards

InTASC Standard	Indicators
3. *Learning Environments* The teacher works with others to create environments that support individual and collaborative learning.	Works with students to establish a positive and supportive learning environment. Understands and uses motivation and engagement to design learning experiences. Develops learning experiences that engage students in collaborative and self-directed learning.
4. *Content Knowledge* The teacher understands the central concepts, tools of inquiry, and structures of the discipline(s) he or she teaches and creates learning experiences that make the discipline accessible and meaningful for learners to ensure mastery of the content.	Selects learning experiences that connect content to national/state/local standards and are relevant to learners. Focuses instruction on essential concepts, inquiry tools, and methods of inquiry in the discipline. Explores the use of new technologies that support and promote student learning. Designs, implements and evaluates differentiated instruction for a diverse and inclusive community of students.
5. *Application of Content* The teacher understands how to connect concepts and use differing perspectives to engage learners in critical thinking, creativity, and collaborative problem solving related to authentic local and global issues.	Understands and uses digital and social media tools for efficient and effective teaching. Models collaboration as an essential learning strategy.
6. *Assessment* The teacher understands and uses multiple methods of assessment to engage learners in their own growth, to monitor learner progress, and to guide the teacher's and learner's decision making.	Uses multiple and appropriate types of assessments to identify needs, develop differentiated learning experiences, and document learning. Uses pre- and postassessments to diagnose, monitor, and document student progress. Uses information obtained from review of student work to plan and modify instruction. Designs formative assessments that match learning objectives to help learners demonstrate knowledge and skills.
7. *Planning for Instruction* The teacher plans instruction that supports every student in meeting rigorous learning goals by drawing upon knowledge of content areas, curriculum, cross-disciplinary skills, and pedagogy, as well as knowledge of learners and the community context.	Selects and creates learning experiences that are appropriate for curriculum goals, relevant to learners, and based upon principle of effective instruction. Evaluates short- and long-term goals and systematically adjusts plans to enhance learning for all students. Uses students' diverse strengths and needs to plan effective instruction. Plans so that adjustments and revisions are based upon student needs and changing circumstances.

FIGURE 7-4 *Portfolio Assessment Tool Using InTASC Standards (continued)*

InTASC Standard	Indicators
8. Instructional Strategies The teacher understands and uses a variety of instructional strategies to encourage learners to develop deep understanding of content areas and their connections, and to build skills to apply knowledge in meaningful ways.	Selects learning experiences that connect content to national/state/local standards and are relevant to learners. Focuses instruction on essential concepts, inquiry tools, and methods of inquiry in the discipline. Explores the use of new technologies that support and promote student learning. Designs, implements, and evaluates differentiated instruction for a diverse and inclusive community of students.
9. Professional Learning and Ethical Practice The teacher engages in ongoing professional learning and uses evidence to continually evaluate his/her practice, particularly the effects of his/her choices and actions on others (learners, families, other professionals, and the community), and adapts practice to meet the needs of each learner.	Integrates classroom observations and analyses of data about students to evaluate the outcomes of teaching and revise practice. Consults professional literature, colleagues, and other professional learning opportunities to advance your own and/or student learning. Engages in professional learning to enhance knowledge and skills. Engages in advocacy for children and the profession and models safe, legal, and ethical behavior.
10. Leadership and Collaboration The teacher seeks appropriate leadership roles and opportunities to take responsibility for student learning, to collaborate with learners, families, colleagues, other school professionals, and community members to ensure learner growth, and to advance the profession.	Participates actively as a part of an instructional team As a continuing learner, seeks opportunities for professional growth. Respects families' norms and expectations and works collaboratively with student and families in meeting goals. Communicates effectively with families, teachers, and resource personnel to foster student learning and success. Shows understanding of the alignment of family, school, and community.

FIGURE 7-4   *Portfolio Assessment Tool Using InTASC Standards (continued)*

What Does a Reflective Narrative Look Like?

A reflective narrative should have a purpose. It is not a mere caption, nor is it a summary of a lesson. It should focus on the processes and the products of your growth. This understanding is so important that it becomes part of your everyday teaching. To help in your understanding of how to write a reflective narrative, we have divided the reflective narrative into several parts that combine knowledge and experience. These parts are shown in Figure 7-5.

- What is the artifact?
- How does the artifact connect to NAEYC Standard (number and letter) and InTASC Standard (number and letter)?
- How does the artifact contribute to my learning?
- In what way does this artifact have a positive impact on student learning?
- Where does this artifact fit within the core cluster of instructional activities (Judging prior learning and background knowledge, Planning instruction, Teaching, Assessing, Analyzing, and Reflecting)?

FIGURE 7-5   *Parts of a Reflective Narrative*

Answering the five questions in Figure 7-5 should aid in your understanding of how to write a narrative. Remember in Chapter 6 when you were asked if you ever taught an unsuccessful lesson and learned from it? If you decided to include such an experience in your portfolio, your reflective narrative might look like this:

> I planned and implemented a reading comprehension lesson for second-grade students. I focused on reading a story and sequencing the events of the story. During the lesson, students listened to the story on CD and then participated in a class discussion about sequencing. The students then engaged in guided practice and independent practice by completing an assessment.
>
> My assessment results showed that I need to reteach the lesson. Therefore, I had to think critically about how to improve my next lesson. I realized that if I had modeled my expectations and used sequencing as an active group activity, my students would have had a better understanding of sequencing. I needed to show, not tell. In my reteaching, I incorporated both of these methods. Assessment results showed that my attempts to increase student understanding the second time was more successful.

Next are exemplary narratives written by 10 different college students. There is at least one example of each NAEYC standard, and all ten InTASC standards are also included. Following some of the narratives, the five questions from Figure 7-5 are answered for you. The answers to these questions show you how to use each of the five parts of a reflective narrative. Any format for these narratives is fine as long as it follows the protocol of your university.

Literacy Case Study

NAEYC Standard 1: Promoting Child Development and Learning. (c) Using developmental knowledge to create healthy, respectful, supportive, and challenging learning environments.

InTASC Standard 1: Learner Development. (f) The teacher identifies readiness for learning, and understands how development in any one area may affect performance in others.

The intention of this case study was for me to learn about student literacy in my classroom. I chose one child who was developing on grade level (according to my mentor-teacher). The case study took place in the classroom for approximately 10 weeks. Each Thursday that I was at my placement, I sat with my student at recess for approximately 15 minutes and worked with her on a particular skill. I started by completing an interest inventory with my student, which gave me ideas about what she liked to do. I then asked her questions about reading by completing the Reading Reflections Interview. This interview included questions about what reading meant to her, like, "What is reading?" The student had to identify what reading was and she also determined whether she was a good reader. The next task I completed was writing samples. I had three samples in order to create benchmarks for her. The first sample was taken in February, the second in March, and the third in April. Each time, I would see if she made any progress. Unfortunately, not much was made.

Another task was the Phonemic Awareness Profile (PAP) test. In this test, the child had to identify syllables, rhyming words, compound words, vowels, diphthongs, consonant blends, and r-controlled vowels. She was also asked to spell words by only hearing the word orally. The child was also asked to substitute sounds and delete sounds as part of this test. The student also orally recited a series of words in the Steiglitz test in order to identify her reading abilities. The student was able to read through second-grade words; however, she reached her frustration at the third-grade word list. After determining the words she could read, the student read three different texts orally to me. I recorded miscues as she read. After each passage was read, the student was asked a series of comprehension questions based on the text. After compiling the information from the tests given to her, I came up with recommendations to help with the skills she had difficulty with. I also recommend books and websites that would help her with literacy.

I placed this artifact under NAEYC Standard 1c because the student was given activities that supported her needs. This also falls under InTASC Standard 1f because I was specifically looking at literacy development.

In doing this case study, I learned that the student I worked with was considered typically developing; however, there were certain skills where she needed more practice. I learned that taking the time to sit with one student builds a relationship. My student was excited to help me complete my homework and she loved telling me the answers. I found out a lot by working with her and I realized that students come in all abilities. I also have learned that differentiating the instruction would be most beneficial due to the varied learners. If I had never done this case study, I would categorize every student the same.

- What is the Artifact?
  A literacy case study.
- How does the Artifact connect to the NAEYC Standard and the InTASC Standard?
  "I placed this artifact under NAEYC Standard 1c because the student was given activities that supported her needs. This also falls under InTASC Standard 1f because I was looking specifically at her literacy development."
- How does the artifact contribute to my learning?
  "I learned that students achieve milestones at different times. The student I worked with was considered typically developing; however, there were certain skills where she needed more practice. I learned that taking the time to sit with one student builds a relationship. I found out a lot by working with her."
- In what way does this artifact have a positive impact on student learning?
  "Students come in all abilities." Differentiating instruction is most beneficial for all learners.
- Where does this artifact fit within the core cluster of instructional activities?
  While this student does not actually answer this question, I would say the core cluster was assessment because she mentions numerous assessments that were used with this child.

Read-Aloud

Spring 2011   ECED 360

NAEYC Standard 1c: Promoting Child Development and Learning: Using developmental knowledge to create healthy, respectful, supportive, and challenging learning environments.

InTASC Standard 8l: The teacher knows when and how to use appropriate strategies to differentiate instruction and engage all students in complex thinking and meaningful tasks.

For this artifact, I led a whole-class read-aloud in my preprimary placement as an assignment for my Early Literacy class. I read the book, *A House for Hermit Crab* by Eric Carle. I put this artifact under NAEYC Standard 1c, Promoting Child Development and Learning, because throughout the read-aloud I was able to support my students' learning according to their needs and abilities. I also felt that this lesson illustrated my use of appropriate strategies to differentiate instruction and engage all students (InTASC 8l).

Before reading I used the students' background knowledge to make predictions about the book. This gave them a purpose for listening (remembering the characters and the job each character had). There are many English for speakers of other languages (ESOL) students in the class. To support their learning, I used felt-board pieces, putting up the characters as we read about them. We also acted out several parts of the book to deepen the students' understanding of the characters. I was able to build the students' vocabulary by using descriptive words.

When I finished reading the book, I left the felt pieces on the board and I asked the students if they could remember the different characters we met and the jobs that they had. My favorite thing that happened was when one of the ESOL students raised his hand to answer what job the pebbles had. He couldn't find the words to answer, but he made the wall with his fingers. It was so great to see that he was able to participate and demonstrate his understanding without expressing it in words.

- What is the artifact?
  A read aloud for Preprimary students
- How does the artifact connect to the NAEYC Standard (number and letter) and the InTASC Standard (number and letter)?
  "I put this artifact under NAEYC Standard 1c, Promoting Child Development and Learning, because throughout the read-aloud, I was able to support my students' learning according to their needs and abilities. I also felt that this lesson illustrated my use of appropriate strategies to differentiate instruction and engage all students (InTASC Standard #8n)."
- How does the artifact contribute to my learning?
  I learned that my ESOL students can "participate and demonstrate understanding without expressing it in words."
- In what way does this artifact have a positive impact on student learning?
  One ESOL student "couldn't find the words to answer, but he made the wall with his fingers. It was so great to see that he was able to participate and demonstrate his understanding without expressing it in words."
- Where does this artifact fit within the core cluster of instructional activities? (judging prior learning and background knowledge, planning instruction, teaching, assessing, analyzing, and reflecting)?
  Judging prior learning and background knowledge: *"I used the students' background knowledge to make predictions about the book"* Planning instruction and Teaching: *"I gave them a purpose of listening . . . I supported their learning I used felt-board pieces . . . we also acted out several parts . . . to deepen understanding of the characters."* Reflecting: *"My favorite thing that happened was . . ."*

Family Literacy Bag

Spring 2011   ECED 360

NAEYC Standard 2: Building Family and Community Relationships. (c) Involving families and communities in their children's development and learning.

InTASC Standard 1: Learner Development. (h) The teacher respects students' differing strengths and needs and is committed to using this information to further each student's development.

The artifact: This artifact, a literacy bag, was created for one student in my kindergarten internship class. The family literacy bag was designed to enhance home-school connections and to encourage part-child interaction while participating in literacy activities. For this project, the student was read three stories and he completed three activities related to the readings. These activities included a parent reading, sequencing a story, writing a sentence about a favorite animal in the book and drawing a picture of it, and classifying ending sounds to given chunks.

Connection to Standards: This artifact fits under NAEYC Standard 2c because it shows the importance of involving families in active learning. It also involves the family community in support of the child's developmental learning. InTASC Standard 1h talks about strengthening the needs of each student. The activities in a literacy bag can be created either to challenge the child or to support areas of needs. In this case, after being in the classroom for several weeks, the activities were chosen to help address this student's needs.

What I learned: Through this assignment, I learned the importance of providing children with opportunities to develop and reinforce their literacy skills as well as strengthening the home-school relationship. The literacy bag provides an excellent opportunity to support students in the classroom. By doing this assignment, I learned that using literacy bags supports my students and allows families to be involved in the learning process. Unlike newsletters, where the teacher does all the communicating, literacy bags provide the opportunity to establish two-way interactions between parents and the teacher.

Impact on student learning: Literacy bags have a beneficial impact on students because they provide opportunities to strengthen possible areas of weakness, to challenge students to develop literacy skills, and to encourage students to become active readers and critical thinkers.

Core cluster: I feel my literacy bag best fits under planning instruction. I planned specific literacy activities aimed to meet the needs of this student.

Field Trip to Green Meadows Farm

NAEYC Standard 2b: Building family and Community Relationships (b) Supporting and engaging families and communities through respectful, reciprocal relationships.

InTASC Standard 10e: Leadership and Collaboration (e) Working with school colleagues, the teacher builds ongoing connections with community resources to enhance student learning and well-being.

This artifact, the result of a field trip planning experience, was completed by three student teachers placed in the same school. We worked together with our mentor teachers to complete all the necessary paperwork and steps in the planning states for a field trip to a local farm. We also were included in the actual field trip experience.

We first communicated with Green Meadows Farm to arrange a trip for 60 first-graders. We also arranged the transportation with a local bus company. We asked parents to volunteer to chaperone, and we included as many as parents who desired to come because we felt the children would learn more from the experience in very small groups. Increased chaperone availability also ensured that the students had ample protection and support while on the trip. Welcoming parents on this field trip also fostered positive relationships among the school, the parents, and the children in the classrooms. It gave parents an opportunity to meet each other and to feel more as if they were part of the school community.

We placed this artifact under NAEYC Standard 2b and InTASC Standard 10e because we engaged families and the community in this field trip. We also worked collaboratively with our mentor-teachers and built a relationship with the personnel at Green Meadows Farm. This trip was a successful, engaging learning experience for all involved.

Parent Interview

Fall 2011   ECED 460

NAEYC Standard 2a: Building Family and Community Relationships: Knowing about and understanding diverse family and community characteristics.

InTASC Standard 2i: Learning Differences: The teacher knows about second language acquisition processes and knows how to incorporate instructional strategies and resources to support language acquisition.

For this artifact, I conducted an interview with the parent of a child who was in an ESOL program. The intention of this interview was to discover in-depth information about the child and his family and their unique linguistic experiences. Questions were asked about both parents' personal and linguistic history, as well as the child's own linguistic experiences. This artifact fits under NAEYC Standard 2, Building Family and Community Relationships, and InTASC Standard 2i, because parent interviews, such as this one, can help to build relationships with students' families and help a teacher understand the unique characteristics of each family.

Through this interview, I was able to obtain a wealth of information about the student that would help me understand his unique approach to learning and his diverse learning needs. From this interview, I learned the importance of seeking information about individual students to enable me to better connect with and serve the child and his family. I also learned what an important role a child's parents can play in getting to know the child! Parents know their child best and they can be a valuable resource for information and suggestions.

Students' school and learning experiences can be improved when their parents and family are invested in and involves as partners in their education. Families can be a useful resource; their advice and insight may prove invaluable in connecting to, encouraging, and enabling students toward success. Taking the initiative to involve a student's family communicates great respect and affirmation to the entire family, and can greatly enhance a student's learning and self-esteem.

Reflective Narrative: Three–Day Math Cycle of Learning

NAEYC Standard 3: Observing, documenting, and assessing to support young children and families.

InTASC Standard 6: The teacher understands and uses multiple methods of assessment to engage learners in their own growth, to monitor learner progress, and to guide the teacher's and learner's decision making.

This artifact took place over a course of three days. The math unit that was taught for this cycle of learning was from the Houghton Mifflin math guide. On Monday, I gave a pre-assessment to determine what the children knew about the skills I would be teaching over the next three days. Day one of my cycle started on Tuesday. I taught a lesson on counting by hundreds in order to reach one thousand. We used place-value models in order to show the values. I used explicit instruction the first half of the lesson and then I gave the students a check. The check determines what they know or don't know from what I had taught them. From the check, I determine if the children need to work with me on the rug, practice the skill problems independently, or need more challenging learning tasks; this was followed by the evaluation from which I could see who struggled and who did not. I determined which students would be in my small group the following day based on the data I had.

The second day of the cycle was counting sets by grouping them into hundreds, tens, and ones. This skill built on the previous day. The children were able to determine the value of the models and write the digits in the correct places. I worked with a small group on grouping by circling sets of different objects. After the evaluation was given this day, I was able to determine who still needed practice based on the data I had.

The third day of the cycle included reading and writing expanded notation in both standard and number form. After explicit instruction, I was able to divide them into groups based on the check once again. I worked with the small low-achieving group on the rug with place value. We rolled dice and placed the value of the digits underneath the correct place (hundreds, tens, ones) that were written on note cards. I chose this group based on the previous day's evaluation. After the evaluation of the skill was given, I went right into a postassessment. The postassessment was based on the skills the students had learned over the three-day period. From that, I determined that each student improved from his or her pre-assessment, which was the objective of this cycle.

This artifact is placed under InTASC Standard 6 because, during these few days, I was able to determine which students needed practice based on their assessment scores. The checks were informative because I was just seeing their progress during the lesson, and the summative assessment was the evaluation given at the end of each lesson. The summative assessment came after more practice work because it gave me and the students more time to focus on the skill. I documented each evaluation and watched the progress of each student (NAEYC standard 3) to ensure that each one was focused and understanding the skill. I needed to support the needs of each learner; therefore, I worked with them one on one, challenged them, or had them practice.

From this cycle, I learned that a few days can make a difference. Some units and/or lessons could take more than three days; however, three days was enough for me to see which students were able to learn the skills and which were not. It was helpful to document each day in order for me to form my small groups. The small groups included the children who struggled the most. In these groups, it is important to have tactiles to aid the children's learning. They stayed engaged and seemed motivated to learn. I noticed that it is hard to have manipulatives for every child; therefore, I determined that it is imperative to pull those tactile learners to the group in order to reach the needs of each and every student. I also incorporated differentiation during independent work. Some students were given more challenging tasks, while others stayed on the specific task to practice.

Math Lesson on Area

NAEYC Standard 4c: Using developmentally effective approaches. Using a broad repertoire of developmentally appropriate teaching/learning approaches.

InTASC Standard 5: Application of Content. (c) The teacher facilitates learners' use of current tools and resources to maximize content learning in varied contexts.

This artifact is a math lesson based on area. The students learned how to find the perimeter of figures the previous day. The focus of this lesson was to find the area of regular and irregular figures in square units. The students first learned what a square unit was and why they were called "square" units. The students started with regular figures. They had to identify the area by counting the squares. As they counted the square units, they wrote the numbers in as they went along in order to avoid miscounting. After the students wrote in the numbers, they took cheese crackers and placed one in each square unit. The students then moved to irregular figures. I first modeled how to count the square units, and then the students practiced. They wrote in the numbers as they counted and then placed cheese crackers to ensure they had counted correctly. After the instruction, I passed out a check form. This is an assessment to see what the students have understood throughout instruction. If the students receive a blue star, they have all of the answers on the check form correct. Then they get their designated paper, which I created from the blue bin, and begin their independent practice. The blue group is the enrichment group. The practice questions I wrote were designed to challenge the students. If the students receive a green star, they either have all correct or they are missing one answer. The green group is the practice group. They get a worksheet that I created from the green bin and work on their practice independently. This group is on level, and they have the same types of questions that we reviewed during instruction. If the students receive a pink star, they meet me on the carpet for reteaching. During this lesson I did not have a reteaching group because everyone had excelled. After I had given the students 10 minutes to complete their practice work, we took the evaluation. The evaluation looked similar to the check questions; however, they were a little different. At the end of the lesson, we played bingo with different shapes, for example, the letter *L*. If the students had bingo, they first needed to tell me the area of the figure.

This artifact was placed under NAEYC 4c and InTASC Standard 5c because I did not use just pencil-and-paper tasks throughout the lesson; I began with an engaging activator. I incorporated manipulatives so the students would be engaged. I also had them play bingo for more learning and fun. This lesson supported different learning styles because I used visual aids and manipulatives.

From this lesson, I learned that it is not bad to skip certain things. I noticed that the students were doing very well throughout the lesson; therefore, I cut out some guided practice to allow more time for independent work and bingo. The students were engaged throughout the lesson, which made the lesson go more smoothly. After reviewing their evaluation scores, I can say I am satisfied with this lesson because all the students received a perfect score.

Techniques for Communications with English Language Learners

NAEYC Standard 4a: Using developmentally effective approaches to connect with children and families. (a) Knowing and understanding effective strategies and tools for early education.

InTASC Standard 3n: Learning environments. (n) The teacher is committed to working with learners, colleagues, families, and communities to establish positive and supportive learning environments.

This assignment consisted of observing, interacting, and applying different communication techniques to a dual-language learner to determine the student's level of language development. I then needed to decide what technique to employ. I observed a 3-year-old boy, who is being raised in a Hindi culture, in a Montessori preschool setting.

This practical experience helped me understand the different stages that an English Language Learner goes through during the language acquisition process, and the importance of providing the correct support. Therefore, observing, documenting, and applying the right techniques are critical to the development of healthy and nurturing environments and to the promotion of language growth.

This project helped me understand the teacher's role in supporting a student learning a second language. The scaffolding had a positive impact on the student's language development and provided him with the tools to support and nurture his language development. Not only did this affect his learning, but it also aided his socialization skills and his self-esteem.

I am committed to developing positive and supportive school environments. I am also devoted to using effective tools and strategies to aid in developing connections with children and families. For these reasons, I placed this artifact under NAEYC Standard 4a and InTASC Standard 3n.

ART HANDBOOK

Spring 2011   **ECED 471**

NAEYC Standard 5: Using content Knowledge to Build Meaningful Curriculum (c) Using their own knowledge, appropriate early learning standards, and other resources to design, implement, and evaluate meaningful, challenging curricula for each child.

InTASC Standard 7: Planning for Instruction. (b) The teacher plans how to achieve student learning goals, choosing appropriate strategies, resources, and materials to differentiate instruction for individuals and groups of students; developing appropriate sequencing of learning experiences; allowing multiple ways to demonstrate knowledge and skills.

This artifact is an art-integrated curriculum handbook including program goals and philosophy; organization of space, materials, and environment; five lesson plans; a list of children's books; and a reflective summary of the experience. The theme I chose was Space because I thought it was engaging for children at the Kindergarten level.

This artifact fits under NAEYC Standard 5c because it is my responsibility to create meaningful lesson plans that meet curriculum standards and to challenge each child individually and the children as a group. This artifact also meets InTASC Standard 7 because I used different art forms to help children develop creative thinking and to produce original work. Encouraging children to think "outside the box" is critical if children are going to learn to use their imaginations to create their own products.

By doing the art-integrated handbook, I learned different ways of integrating varied art forms into the general curriculum, thus making the activities more dynamic and creative. Children learn differently from one another, so when activities are presented in several ways, learning seems to be more accessible and less rigid. Some students are more artistic than others, and by providing them the opportunity to express themselves through art rather than worksheets, their window of learning automatically expands. Also, I see art integration as a benefit for those students who have poor communication skills because it is a means by which they can express their feelings and show their knowledge.

Transportation Lesson in JPTAAR* Format

Spring 2011   **ECED 341**

NAEYC Standard 5: Using Content Knowledge to Build Meaningful Curriculum. (c) Using their own knowledge, appropriate early learning standards and other resources to design, implement, and evaluate meaningful, challenging curricula for each child.

InTASC Standard 4: Content Knowledge. (a) The teacher effectively uses multiple representations and explanations of concepts that capture key ideas in the discipline, guide learners through learning progressions, and promote each learner's achievement of content standards.

This artifact is a large-group JPTAAR lesson plan introducing the topic of transportation. This lesson was taught in my preprimary internship in a Head Start classroom at Twinbrook Elementary. I put this artifact under NAEYC Standard 5c and InTASC Standard 4a because I built this lesson around the state curriculum standard 3.0 Geography, b. identify ways in which people travel to various places in the community. Throughout the lesson, I created personal connections to students and I tapped their prior knowledge. I also used a variety of age-appropriate representations of the topic (pictures, books, promethium board) to explain the concepts so that each student would reach the lesson objective to identify three or more types of transportation successfully.

    I feel that this was the most successful lesson plan I have written and implemented thus far. From feedback and input from my mentor and supervisor, I was able to write a truly integrated lesson plan. I successfully integrated math and art into a social studies objective. After planning and executing this lesson, I feel much more confident in my ability to create effective and meaningful lessons.

    Throughout the lesson, I involved all of the students. I supported and extended their prior knowledge of transportation. I was also able to extend the oral-language skills for several of the second-language learners by presenting the types of transportation using several different visual representations. All students met the objective.

*JPTAAR stands for "Judges prior learning, Planning, Teaching, Assessing, Analysis, and Reflection."

Videotape Reflection

NAEYC Standard 6: Becoming a Professional. (c) Engaging in continuous, collaborative learning to inform practice.

InTASC Standard 9: Reflection and Continuous Growth (n) The teacher sees herself as a learner, continuously seeking opportunities for professional growth.

I had the opportunity to videotape my teaching during my primary internship course. I reflect on my teaching after every lesson, but viewing a videotape of my teaching gave me new perspectives. My own and others' evaluations of my performance may not provide me with a complete view of the multiple interacting influences occurring in the classroom, but a videotape of it provides a wider range of views that contains much objective information. I noticed aspects of the classroom environment, such as student engagement, that I wasn't fully aware of while teaching. I also noted other aspects of instruction, such as my behavior management strategies and tone of voice.

This artifact meets NAEYC Standard 6c because I used a videotape in conjunction with my mentor's and my own observations to gain a comprehensive view of my work. I feel like a well-prepared teacher-candidate because I allowed my practice to be influenced by knowledgeable, reflective, and critical perspectives. Observing myself on videotape provided me with a new perspective on my teaching. I found I was able to make adjustments to my lesson content, relationships with students, and classroom management to make a positive impact on student learning. This artifact fits under InTASC Standard 9n because I recognized my responsibility to engage in continual professional development. I combined my videotape observations with analysis of student work to evaluate my teaching. Throughout the reflection, I described ways in which I would revise my teaching practices to enhance student learning. This videotape has helped me to understand important aspects of how I deliver instruction and interact with children during my teaching.

- What is the artifact?
  A videotape of me teaching.
- How does the artifact connect to the NAEYC Standard or INTASC Standard?
  "I used a videotape in conjunction with my mentor's and my own observations to gain a comprehensive view of my work. I feel like a well-prepared teacher-candidate because I allowed my practice to be influenced by knowledgeable, reflective, and critical perspectives. Observing myself on videotape provided me with a new perspective on my teaching. I found I was able to make adjustments to my lesson content, relationships with students, and classroom management to make a positive impact on student learning."
- How does the artifact contribute to my learning?
  "I recognized my responsibility to engage in continual professional development. I combined my videotape observations with analysis of student work to evaluate my teaching."
- In what way does this artifact have a positive impact on student learning?
  "Throughout the reflection, I described ways in which I would revise my teaching practices to enhance student learning."
- Where does this artifact fit within the core cluster of instructional activities (Judging prior learning and background knowledge, Planning instruction, Teaching, Assessing, Analyzing, and Reflecting)?
  Teaching, Assessing, Analyzing, and Reflecting "This video tape has helped me to understand important aspects of how I deliver instruction and interact with children during my teaching."

As part of your coursework, you may be asked to write a reflective narrative for various assignments. This is good practice! Writing narratives as you complete assignments will keep them fresh and keep you from falling into the "all narratives sound alike" syndrome. Nothing is more boring for a portfolio assessor than to read the exact the same wording in narrative after narrative. Figure 7-6 is a rubric that can be used to grade reflective narratives. The criterion for grading may also help you in writing your narrative.

Points	5	4	3	2	1
Description of artifact	A well-written, clear description of the artifact that includes what the intern did; where, when, and why she or he did it; and the purpose of the activity.	A good description of the artifact that includes what the intern did; where, when, and why she or he did it; and the purpose of the activity.	Artifact is described satisfactorily but may not include what the intern did; where, when, and why she or he did it; and the purpose of the activity.	The artifact is not well described and does not include what the intern did; where, when, and why she or he did it; and the purpose of the activity.	The artifact is poorly described and does not include what the intern did; where, when, and why she or he did it; and the purpose of the activity.
Rationale for NAEYC/InTASC	Exemplary rationale and connection to standards	Good rationale and connection to standards	Satisfactory rationale and connection to standards	Some rationale and some connection to standards	Little or no rationale and little connection to standards.
Impact on my growth	Exemplary demonstration of intern's growth and what was learned.	Above average demonstration of intern's growth and what was learned.	Satisfactory demonstration of intern's growth and what was learned.	Little demonstration of intern's growth and what was learned.	Little or no explanation of intern's growth or what was learned.
Impact on student learning	Exemplary demonstration/explanation of student growth, supported with data.	Competent demonstration and explanation of student growth; supporting data included.	Satisfactory demonstration and/or explanation of student growth; some supporting data included.	Some demonstration or explanation of student growth. Little or no supporting data.	Poor or no demonstration of how students grew as a result of this artifact.
Relationship to core clusters	Exemplary demonstration of planning and teaching, assessment, analysis, and/or reflection.	Competent demonstration of planning and teaching, assessment, analysis, and/or reflection.	Satisfactory demonstration of planning and teaching, assessment, analysis, and/or reflection.	Unsatisfactory demonstration of planning and teaching, assessment, analysis, and/or reflection.	Poor demonstration of planning and teaching, assessment, analysis, and/or reflection.

FIGURE 7-6 *Rubric for Grading Reflective Narratives*

ACTIVITY 7-1

Go back to the sample narratives provided in this chapter and pick one of the ten examples that is not followed by the five components of a narrative. For the sample narrative that you select, identify the five components of a reflective narrative yourself.

ACTIVITY 7-2

Read the reflective narrative below. Provide the evidence needed for a complete and effective reflection.

NAEYC Standard 1: Promoting child development and learning

InTASC Standard 1: Learner development

This artifact is a case study of a typically developing 2-year-old boy. It was completed during the fall of 2010 for ECED 315. In this case study, I observed this child for 5 hours, watching and observing his social, linguistic, cognitive, emotional, and physical development. I learned that this child meets all benchmarks of a typical developing child. This case study contributes to my professional growth as an early childhood educator because

_____

_____

As a teacher who knows how to carefully observe the whole child, I would make a positive impact on student learning because

_____

_____

I think that this artifact belongs in NAEYC Standard 1 and InTASC Standard 1 because

_____

_____

This observation will help me as a teacher because

_____

_____

The core cluster that this artifact meets is

_____

_____

_____ because _____

ACTIVITY 7-3

Pick one of your artifacts and write a reflective narrative, incorporating the five components presented in this chapter. Have a classmate or instructor review your reflective narrative for clarity, written expression, and adherence to reflective narrative requirements.

Summary

You have learned in this chapter what a reflective narrative is and how to write an effective and persuasive one. You know that writing your narrative demands thought. Your narrative needs to extend your personal philosophy, provide a rationale for what you did and why you did it, clearly articulate why this artifact fits into the standard(s) you selected for it, and explain how it contributes to student learning and your own growth as a teacher. You know that it needs to include five components:

- What is the artifact?
- Why did I put this artifact in this standard?
- How does this artifact contribute to my learning?
- How does this artifact contribute to student learning?
- Where does this artifact fit within the core cluster of activities in the classroom?

Remember that every narrative should not sound the same. Vary how you respond to the five necessary elements. The length of your narrative is unimportant as long as you address the primary questions. However, a good rule of thumb is to keep your narrative to one page.

 Suggested Website

e-Portfolio Information Part 3
facstaff.uww.edu/eppsv/portfolio/portfolio_index.htm

 References

Council of Chief State School Officers (2011, April). Interstate Teacher Assessment and Support Consortium (InTASC) Model Core Teaching Standards: A Resource for State Dialogue. Washington, DC: Author. Retrieved from www.ccsso.org/InTASC_Model_Core_Teaching_Standards_2011.pdf

NAEYC Standards for Early Childhood Professional Preparation Programs (2009). Position Statement. Retrieved from www.naeyc.org

chapter 8

· ·

The Collection Phase

A purposeful collection of work that documents your experiences, activities, training, preparation, classroom skills, and accomplishments is an important part of building an effective portfolio. This task involves gathering, sorting, and storing examples of what you are doing in college classes and in early childhood classrooms, and what you have already done to illustrate your potential as a future early childhood educator. This chapter gives you suggestions about collecting, cataloging, and saving evidence that you might eventually want to use in your showcase or interview portfolio. Our advice is to save everything!

How Does the Collection Phase Work?

You have already learned that the portfolio process is ongoing. The collection and developmental portfolios are two types of portfolios defined in Chapter 1. They could be considered various levels of the gathering process because the emphasis of a collection portfolio is amassing a wide assortment of artifacts that record your potential as an early childhood educator. A developmental portfolio is focused more on the work you do to affect children and your ongoing growth toward becoming a teacher. An artifact you felt was appropriate as a freshman may seem inappropriate as you mature and develop. However, at each level of your advancement, maybe at the end of each semester or during each summer, collect and file evidence of your accomplishments, skills, assignments, internships, special training, journals, workshops, and other important activities in your life that pertain to your knowledge of and involvement with young children. We recommend that you accumulate evidence from any of your classes, training, activities, hobbies, employment, and service that are relevant to you becoming a teacher. At this point, it is better to have too much than too little. Save hard copies of all your computer-generated documents. Collecting materials for an electronic portfolio is no different than amassing written materials, except that you will save all files on a zip disk, travel drive, or DVD.

What Artifacts Do I Want to Include?

Selecting artifacts for a portfolio is an individual decision. This is where you can use your own creativity and sensitivity to decide what is important to showcase you as a future teacher. Descriptions of possible artifacts are included on the following pages so that you may make better decisions about their use. Each artifact is defined as it relates to early childhood education, and the skills and dispositions that each artifact may encompass are clarified (Campbell et al., 2011). We recommend that you go back to Chapter 6 and view Figures 6-1, 6-2, and 6-3 for ideas of artifacts that are appropriate for a portfolio. Figure 6-6 provides six artifacts that use both NAEYC and InTASC Standards; this cross-reference guide may be very helpful if your university uses both sets of standards. These charts should help you collect and categorize artifacts.

Action research: Action research takes place in the classroom and is aimed at improving classroom instruction, student learning, or your own practice.

Anecdotal records: Anecdotal records are notes taken during classroom observations or while teaching that may pertain to children's intellectual, social, physical, or emotional development. They are valid assessment procedures in early childhood education.

Annotated bibliography: An annotated bibliography provides a study of children's literature and the criteria that makes a quality book for 3- to 5-year-old children. This involves planning, diversity, and use of multiple resources.

Article summaries or critiques: A summary of an article in a professional journal is often a class assignment. When using it as a portfolio artifact, choose an article to critique that shows your ability to analyze professional material.

Assessments: Any artifact that measures children's performances would be considered assessment. Explain whether you are assessing children's performance, diagnosing progress, or using the assessment to modify instruction.

Attendance at PTA meetings, school board meetings, or other school functions: Your own professional development is important. Attending school functions such as back to school night, PTA meetings, or parent-teacher conferences is one way to meet other professionals and families informally.

Attendance at conferences, workshops, and/or seminars: Joining professional organizations and attending conferences, workshops, and/or seminars provide opportunities to enhance your own professional development. Meeting other dedicated teachers and administrators in a professional setting often provides you with new ideas and a fresh approach.

Author study: The study of one particular author over a period of time involves planning, implementing, and assessing student knowledge. This can provide motivation and use of a variety of resources to engage all learners.

Back to school night: Back to school night is a chance for parents to visit their children's classrooms and hear about the curriculum. This opportunity allows teachers to establish communication with families about procedures, routines, homework, and volunteering in the classroom.

Behavior management plan: You may need to develop a behavior modification or management plan to control and monitor a student's behavior. This plan could include strategies such as changes to the environment, positive reinforcements, support for acceptable classroom behavior, and consequences for unacceptable classroom behavior. Normally this plan is shared with school administrators, parents, and the student. Consequences for failure to adhere to the plan are de-lineated. This artifact provides documentation of your ability to manage student behavior.

Bulletin board displays: Bulletin boards are creative displays in hallways or class-rooms showcasing children's work samples or highlighting a particular topic of interest or study. They can be used to motivate children, to collaborate with others, and to motivate student learning.

Case study: A case study consists of a series of child observations focusing on one or more developmental domains, usually documenting one child. This artifact shows knowledge of child development and could address typical or atypical development.

Child study: A child study consists of a series of reading and writing assessments about a child that provide information for daily instruction. This type of artifact may help you better understand diverse learners, child development, and using assessment and differentiation to plan instruction.

Classroom management plan: A classroom management plan is designed by the teacher to support student learning, instruction, and behavior through docu-mented routines and classroom procedures.

Community involvement: There are many ways to involve the community in aca-demic activities and curriculum. Community resources can be used to foster student learning.

Conferencing with families: Parent-teacher conferences provide in-depth exchanges of information. While teachers can explain aspects of the curriculum, families can provide valuable information about children's special interests, concerns, and background.

Computer programs analysis: This type of assignment allows you to explore and ana-lyze technology programs for young children. This artifact involves knowledge of communication and technology, and could include specific ways to integrate technology in the classroom.

Content-specific units: Sometimes known as themed units or projects, children's ideas and interests are investigated while teachers promote learning using organization, exploration, modeling, scaffolding, questioning, and documen-tation. These units demonstrate that children can reflect on what they have discovered.

Cooperative learning: Cooperative learning is a method of classroom instruction in which students work collaboratively in small groups to examine, experience, and understand a topic of study or to solve a problem. Using this tool in a lesson plan provides evidence of your ability to manage and motivate students.

Culturally responsive instruction: Instruction that is culturally responsive requires knowledge of cultural values, learning styles, and achievements of all ethnic groups. Curriculum, instruction, and assessment are embedded in multicultural contexts, which promote academic success for all. When you model acceptance, caring, and mutual respect for all, you demonstrate your disposition to plan instruction that builds partnerships with the families and communities of your students.

Curriculum plans: Knowing the curriculum and planning daily, as well as long term, are essential requirements for early childhood teachers. Connecting national, state, and local standards and linking plans to children's prior knowledge are key concepts.

Cycles of learning: A two-, three-, or five-day (or longer) cycle of learning uses one primary objective that is both measurable and observable. The cycle involves awareness of prior knowledge through the use of a pre-assessment. Daily planning and teaching, as well as both formative and summative assessment, analysis of data gathered, and reflection, are required in a cycle of learning. Student work samples and cumulative data graphs or charts provide evidence of the learning that took place.

Data analysis of student learning: The collection and analysis of objective, empirical data about student learning can be a powerful artifact that provides evidence of your knowledge of human development, learning, assessment and about your ability to adapt instruction to individual needs. Your ability to plan interactions to improve learning can be recorded through thorough data collection and analysis.

Differentiated instruction: Differentiated instruction adjusts both teaching and assessing to the wide-ranging needs of all learners. You may present information using numerous modalities, multiple intelligences, and/or assistive or other types of technology to meet the needs of all the students in your class. You may connect key concepts to students' prior knowledge and experiences. A range of assessment types may address specific learning differences. Some lesson plans may include special accommodations for individuals, small groups, or whole-group instruction. Your ability to design meaningful lessons that address cultural diversity and individual differences demonstrates your ability to adapt instruction.

Ethics paper: The purpose of an ethics paper is to identify an ethical issue or dilemma, familiarize yourself with NAEYC's Code of Ethics, develop an action plan using the code as your professional reference, and cite specific ideals and principles from the code to support your plan. This artifact could illustrate collaboration, communication, and/or identification of professional literature to advance professional development and growth.

Field trip plans: Every community has endless possibilities for learning. Incorporating field trips can make learning real to children, For field trips to be successful, however, advance planning and organization are crucial. This assignment involves planning, organization, and reflection.

Individual education plan (IEP): An individual education plan (IEP) is an assessment, intervention, and evaluation plan designed with school staff members to support children who need specific modifications in their daily instruction. IEPs involve administrators, specialists, and families in addition to the teacher and the child.

Integrating technology: Lessons that integrate technology meaningfully into the classroom may require you to consult professionals who are knowledgeable about technology. The use of technology helps involve students in active, hands-on learning. Ideas include the use of computers, promethium boards, photography, and Kidspiration and other soft ware appropriate for young children.

Interviews: Interviews can capture many types of interesting data. For example, interviewing parents whose first language is not English may help you understand their perspectives on school and learning. Interviews with seasoned teachers, administrators, students, caregivers, or parents can be viable artifacts. Whether the interview is a class assignment or part of a larger project, be sure to include the purpose of the interview, a copy of the questions asked and the answers, and a summary and an analysis of the interview.

Journal entries: Journaling supports a reflective orientation that relates theory to practice because you continuously assess your teaching; consider a variety of viewpoints and perspectives; and understand the personal, social, political, and moral implications of your instruction decisions. Journal entries should help you evaluate and reflect on your teaching experiences and chronicle your growth from student to preservice teacher.

Lesson plans: A lesson plan is a format or script that includes national, state, and local standards; goals and objectives; a list of materials; a list of procedures; closure; and assessments. This plan shows that you understand key ideas, methods of inquiry, content, students' developmental levels, and student differences. Early childhood education lesson plans should be age-appropriate and developmentally appropriate.

Licensure or certification documentation: Documentation of licensure or certification indicates that you have met certain standards. These documents could be state or district standards that provide requirements and certification for teachers and other professionals in education.

List of websites: Making a list of websites that will help you as a teacher could be a viable artifact. You can find websites that include lesson plans, assessments, standards, newsletters, bulletin board ideas, and a variety of other useful topics.

Literacy bags: A literacy bag is collection of developmentally appropriate activities to support early literacy development at home. This activity encourages home–school connections. They can also be geared for a specific child.

Literacy study: A literacy study looks at best practices in balanced reading instruction. A literacy study could involve planning, assessing, connecting with families, motivation, and integration with technology.

Newsletters: Newsletters, in print or online form, provide regular written communication that keeps families in touch with what is going on in the classroom. Translating newsletters into the students' native languages obviously enhances the communication and thus the connection between families and the classroom.

Observations: Observations involve watching children in their school or day-care environment for a specific purpose (for example, to observe peer and caregiver interactions). There could be many reasons for observation, such as collecting data, watching a specific child do a particular task, assessing, documenting developmental milestones, and designing instruction to meet individual needs.

Organizers: Visual and graphic organizers, semantic maps, and story maps are tools that help some children choose ideas, organize their thoughts and writing, elaborate on a topic, and edit written material. Creating a content organizer could document your knowledge of a particular subject area and your skill in using an effective instructional strategy.

Pacing guides: Pacing guides are instruction or curriculum guides that implement instruction in a particular sequence and/or a certain time frame. They might provide you with a way to document efficient use of instructional time.

Parental involvement: Activities that are designed to build the home–school partnership and parent support are important in early childhood classrooms. Many different artifacts could meet this goal.

Parent projects: Parent projects can vary from writing a newsletter to developing a home–school collaborative project. We know that when parents are involved in the learning process, children do better in school. This type of artifact demonstrates effective communication between families and teachers to foster student learning and student success, and demonstrates professional use of oral and written language skills.

Peer critique: Feedback from peers is one way to grow professionally. A supportive and cooperative critique that is directed at improving teaching and learning might demonstrate collaboration.

Philosophy of education statement: The philosophy of education statement provides your personal beliefs about how children learn and how you as an educator can support the development of the whole child. This document provides viewers with your knowledge of content, child development, and your ability to reflect.

Pictures and photographs: Some artifacts, like a bulletin board you designed, cannot be put into your portfolio. Photographs that show active learning in progress are terrific artifacts. Field trips, learning centers, prop boxes, literacy bags, and other classroom activities can be captured in pictures and photographs. In e-portfolios, film clips and sound bites can be impressive artifacts.

Pre- and postassessments: Pre-assessments are used to assess children's prior knowledge before teaching, and postassessments show knowledge growth after a unit of study or a lesson has been taught. Together, they document student learning. Assessments can also be used to diagnose, monitor, and evaluate progress.

Professional development plans: Professional development plans are individualized plans that support instruction specifically to improve the pedagogy of teachers. They can be used to assess your own development and/or improve weak areas of the planning-teaching-assessing process.

Professional organizations: Professional growth continues when you join and actively participate in organizations that support your professional interests and teaching. For example, many early childhood educators join the National Association for the Education of Young Children (NAEYC) or the Council for Exceptional Children (CEC). Participation in outside professional activities can improve your practice.

Prop boxes: Prop boxes are often used during an integrated theme unit. They include authentic, hands-on materials for a specific age group that stimulate dramatic play, diversity, learning, and literacy development. This artifact could document your understanding of child development; connections to national, state, or local standards; a positive classroom environment; your use of a variety of materials to meet students' needs; and your ability to help students assume responsibility for their own learning.

Reflective writing: Similar to journals and self-evaluation, reflective writing allows you to combine educational theory with field experience teaching.

Research papers: Study and research related to a specific topic or learning domain give you a knowledge base from which to grow.

Review of an article from an early childhood journal: Reading and reviewing professional articles demonstrate your use of professional literature. Professional journals can help you develop professionally, revise practice, advance student learning, and/or advance your own learning.

Rubrics: Rubrics are used to measure student performance or as tools for self-assessment. Rubrics show the gradation of levels of proficiency, assign a score to each level, and contain a description of the criteria needed to attain that score. An example of rubrics you designed and a description of how you used them to assess student work, including student work samples and their scores, would exhibit your ability to determine student accomplishment on a specific assignment or project.

Samples of student work: Children's work samples document your ability to link student learning to prior knowledge, to meet students' needs, to encourage critical thinking and problem solving, to illustrate outcomes, and to document student achievement.

Samples of work showing a progression of ideas: Student work samples collected over time in a particular content area such as reading, writing, and/or math can be used to plan and modify instruction. Including such samples in your portfolio illustrates your ability to prepare and adapt instruction to meet the needs of your students.

Self-evaluation: Self-evaluation is a type of reflective practice in which you describe and document your development during a particular time frame. It might ask you to review course objectives to address your growth over time, or simply to evaluate a lesson or activity that you implemented in your field placement and identify strengths and weaknesses in the lesson.

Service learning: Service learning is a form of experiential education that involves a blending of community service activities with the academic curriculum. As you move from student to teacher, service learning can provide you with opportunities to develop responsibility, caring, giving, democratic character, integrity, and authentic problem solving.

Teaching evaluations from mentors or supervisors: Evaluations from your mentor or your supervisor provide you with constructive feedback about all areas of teaching and learning. Evaluations can be valuable additions to portfolio because they demonstrate your growth.

Teacher-made materials: Teacher-made materials can include, but are not limited to, games, manipulatives, puppets, books, charts, teaching aids, posters, and many more. Often these types of artifacts document your creativity, active learning, and the use of different educational strategies.

Thematic units: Thematic units are units of study designed around one theme, idea, or project that integrate many content areas. Use of this type of unit can illustrate long- and short-term planning; connecting national, state, and local standards to content; your ability to plan active and developmentally appropriate instruction; and the use of authentic assessment to document student learning.

Theme bags: Theme bags are designed to support instructional themes through the use of hands-on activities. Often these bags are taken home, thereby providing a home–school connection. They are also one way to document hands-on learning in various content areas.

Videotapes of you teaching: Videotaping is a tool to improve your own teaching. It allows you to revisit your teaching and focus on a wider range of instructional decisions and student interactions with each repeated viewing. By viewing and critiquing yourself or others, you can reflect on the whole experience and thus develop a clearer sense of style, strengths, and areas for development.

Volunteer experiences: A document that describes your volunteer experiences and service in a particular preschool, school, or community center would be an artifact that focuses on the importance of the school–community connection and collaboration.

The items in the preceding list were drawn from many sources (Bullock & Hawk, 2011; Campbell et. al., 2011; Jones & Shelton, 2011; Rieman & Okrasinski, 2010). You can do additional research to discover even more artifacts for inclusion in your portfolio.

Sorting Your Artifacts

Find a way to organize and categorize the documents that you have chosen to save. This task will be unique to you because there are many ways to arrange your portfolio. You may want to organize items around a theme, NAEYC or InTASC standards, content areas, or grade level. You could categorize them chronologically by year or course. You may want to develop your own unique categories that are meaningful to you, like technology, group projects, educational theory, lesson plans. No matter how you decide to organize your materials, keeping a checklist similar to those suggested in Chapter 6 is a good idea. Checklists allow you easy access to your artifacts.

Storing Your Artifacts

Once again, how you choose to store your artifacts is up to you. Putting artifacts for each NAEYC or InTASC atandard in a file folder is one way to organize your potential pieces of work. If you have a large collection of items, a box for each category might work even better. Whether you are working on a paper or an electronic portfolio, it is wise to save hard copies of all your work, as well as backing up all computer-generated documents.

ACTIVITY 8-1

Use Figure 8-1 to chart and categorize the artifacts you have collected to date. Be sure to collect a variety of artifacts.

Assignment or Experience	Date	NAEYC Standard Met

FIGURE 8-1 *Chart for Collecting and Categorizing Artifacts*

Summary

The collection phase includes gathering, sorting, and safely storing materials amassed during your undergraduate coursework. Even if particular courses or instructors do not ask to see specific artifacts for the professional portfolio, it is important that you continue to add, organize, and store your course assignments and work from your internship experiences. Remember this is an ongoing process.

Suggested WebSites

Collecting artifacts for your portfolio:

http://tqe.siu.edu/aud/Your%20TEP%20Portfolio/ 2%20Artifacts.htm

www.colby-sawyer.edu

www4.uwm.edu/soe/cpe/eport_artifacts.cfm

olms.cte.jhu.edu/olms/data/resource/529/ DPInteractiveTour.swf

www.ehow.com

www.kean.edu/~tpc/portfolio/portfolio.html

 References

Bullock, A. A., & Hawk, P. P. (2011). *Developing a teaching portfolio: A guide for preservice and practicing teachers* (3rd ed.). Upper Saddle River, NJ: Pearson.

Campbell, D. M., Cignetti, P. B., Melenyzer, B. J., Nettles, D. H., & Wyman, R. M. (2011). *How to develop a professional portfolio: A manual for teachers* (5th ed.). Boston, MA: Pearson Education.

Jones, M., & Shelton, M. (2011). *Developing your portfolio: Enhancing your learning and showing your stuff. A guide for the early childhood student or professional* (2nd ed.). New York: Routledge.

Rieman, P. L., & Okrasinski, J. (2010). *Creating your teaching portfolio* (3rd ed.). Upper Saddle River, NJ: Pearson Education.

chapter 9

The Final Phase
Preparing and Presenting Your Professional Portfolio

The portfolio review and presentation is a powerful tool for the preservice intern as well as for the assessors. It illustrates tangible evidence of your ability to take on the responsibility of teaching and caring for young children. One goal of this chapter is to help you prepare for the interview process and present your professional portfolio as a summative assessment of your preservice teaching career.

By now you have collected a large, viable selection of artifacts. Your job now is to refine them into a polished, balanced showcase portfolio that presents you as a skilled early childhood candidate who meets all NAEYC Standards for Early Childhood Professional Preparation Programs and InTASC Model Core Teaching Standards. Your portfolio is evidence of your learning and growth throughout your undergraduate early childhood program. The personal background section of your portfolio should include your personal documents (see Chapter 4 for a review). The professional background section is the specialized part of your portfolio that illustrates your understanding of what it means to be a teacher of young children. This section should include three to five artifacts under each of the six NAEYC standards, correlated with the 2011 InTASC principles. The appendix to your portfolio contains any additional artifacts that you want to include, like photographs, letters from parents, and other memorabilia. These items do not need a reflective narrative, but a caption describing the item is highly suggested. All of your examples throughout your entire portfolio should now be of the highest quality. They should all be clean copies edited for proper spelling, punctuation, and grammar. Next, we will look at ways to help you select the most appropriate examples of the work you have done.

Choosing the Best Artifacts for Your Showcase Portfolio

You have been developing and working on your portfolio throughout your program, so you have undoubtedly received feedback and constructive criticism from professors and instructors. In every class you have taken, you have received indications of the work that is high quality. This is the kind of work that you want to include at this level.

You might consult peers, mentor-teachers, or people outside the education field to look over your final choices. Certainly, those familiar with NAEYC and InTASC standards can give you advice and opinions about what they think should be included. But parents and friends who are not in the field can proofread your material and can give you an outsider's opinion.

As you progressed in your program, you took courses that focused exclusively on early childhood content, and you engaged in longer and more extensive field placements. These two components helped you to acquire and apply knowledge of child development, content knowledge, meaningful curriculum, learning environments, learning styles, application of content, developmentally effective approaches, connecting with families, diversity, technology, planned instruction, classroom organization and management, formal and informal assessment, instructional strategies, collaboration, reflection and growth, and professional development. At the heart of the selection process is identifying documentation of best practices, developmentally appropriate active learning, and well-written reflections. These documents will result in an authentic assessment medium—your portfolio. As you engage in your final capstone experience, often known as student teaching, you take on increased responsibilities for teaching in diverse, inclusive, and technologically advanced environments.

While all portfolios create a context for feedback about teaching experiences, the showcase portfolio provides a helpful formative assessment and an excellent tool for self-evaluation because it promotes reflecting on goals, areas of strength and weaknesses, and developing rationales for the chosen selections. The purposes of the summative assessment include presenting a personal portrait of yourself; chronicling your professional development; tailoring your presentation to the use of specific standards; providing multiple sources of evidence, and providing verification that, over time, the standards have been met.

The final requirement for graduation at many institutions is the completed showcase portfolio, presented to a panel of practicing teachers, administrators, and/or faculty members during your final semester. This sharing is a powerful culminating activity whereby you, the intern, celebrate the importance of your work with seasoned professionals who provide you with feedback. Figure 9-1 is a sample portfolio assessment rating sheet similar to many used at institutions of higher learning.

Determining the Appropriateness of Your Artifacts

Constantino and DeLorenzo (2009, p. 49) provide some excellent questions for you to consider as you make the important decisions about what artifacts to select for your final portfolio. Answering these questions will help you determine whether the document is worthy of inclusion:

- Do the artifacts align with the purpose of your portfolio?
- Do the artifacts support a performance standard or theme?
- Are the artifacts credible and do they support progress toward your professional growth, learning, and goals?
- Do the artifacts provide substance and meaning to your portfolio?
- If a particular artifact were eliminated, would it detract from the credibility of your portfolio?

NAEYC Standard	Explanations/Indicators	Comments	Rating
1. Promoting Child Development and Learning 1a: Knowing and understanding young children's characteristics and needs. 1b: Knowing and understanding the multiple influences on development and learning. 1c: Using developmental knowledge to create healthy, respectful, supportive, and challenging learning environments.	Shows knowledge of typical and atypical growth and development. Designs instruction that meets learner's current needs based on age, ability, development, learning style, readiness, culture, social group, and/or values. Understands learning theory, human development, cultural diversity, and individual differences.		
2. Building Family and Community Relationships 2a: Knowing about and understanding diverse family and community characteristics. 2b: Supporting and engaging families and communities through respectful, reciprocal relationships. 2c: Involving families and communities in their children's development and learning.	Identifies and uses community resources to foster student learning and success. Communicates effectively with families, teachers, and resource personnel to foster student learning and success. Shows understanding of the alignment of family, school, and community.		
3. Observing, Documenting, and Assessing to Support Young Children and Families 3a: Understanding the goals, benefits, and uses of assessment. 3b: Knowing about assessment partnerships with families and with professional colleagues. 3c: Knowing about and using observation, documentation, and other appropriate assessment tools and approaches.	Uses multiple and appropriate types of assessments to identify needs, develop differentiated learning experiences, and document learning. Uses pre- and postassessments to diagnose, monitor, and document student progress. Uses information obtained from review of student work to plan and modify instruction. Designs formative assessments that match learning objectives to help learners demonstrate knowledge and skills.		
4. Using Developmentally Effective Approaches to Connect with Children and Families 4a: Understanding positive relationships and supportive interactions as the foundation of their work with children. 4b: Knowing and understanding effective strategies and tools for early education. 4c: Using a broad repertoire of developmentally appropriate teaching/learning approaches. 4d: Reflecting on their own practice to promote positive outcomes for each child.	Supports and expands learners' communication through speaking, listening, reading, writing, and other media. Uses appropriate strategies and resources to adapt to the needs of individual students (e.g., prior knowledge, interests, developmental differences). Integrates technological tools to engage students, families, and/or colleagues. Respects families' norms and expectations and works collaboratively with students and families in meeting goals.		

FIGURE 9-1 *Portfolio Assessment Rating Sheet*

NAEYC Standard	Explanations/Indicators	Comments	Rating
5. Using Content Knowledge to Build Meaningful Curriculum 5a: Understanding content knowledge and resources in academic disciplines. 5b: Knowing and using the central concepts, inquiry tools, and structures of content areas or academic disciplines. 5c: Using their own knowledge, appropriate early learning standards, and other resources to design, implement, and evaluate meaningful, challenging curricula for each child.	Selects learning experiences that connect content to national/state/local standards and are relevant to learners. Focuses instruction on essential concepts, inquiry tools, and methods of inquiry in the discipline. Explores the use of new technologies that support and promote student learning. Designs, implements, and evaluates differentiated instruction for a diverse and inclusive community of students.		
6. Becoming a Professional 6a: Identifying and involving oneself with the early childhood field. 6b: Knowing about and upholding ethical standards and other professional guidelines. 6c: Engaging in continuous, collaborative learning to inform practice. 6d: Integrating knowledgeable, reflective, and critical perspectives on early education. 6e: Engaging in informed advocacy for children and the profession.	Integrates classroom observations and analyses of data about students to evaluate the outcomes of teaching and revise practice. Consults professional literature, colleagues, and other professional learning opportunities to advance your own and/or student learning. Engages in professional learning to enhance knowledge and skills. Engages in advocacy for children and the profession and models safe, legal, and ethical behavior. Participates actively as part of an instructional team.		

FIGURE 9-1 *Portfolio Assessment Rating Sheet (continued)*

Martin-Kniep (1999, p. 6) suggests that teacher candidates assemble professional portfolios with no more than five items in each section. These items should represent the following outcomes:

- The ability to communicate effectively with a variety of audiences.
- The ability to reflect on one's practice and to set goals or further one's professional development.
- The ability to identify and use effective curriculums or programs to meet the needs of different kinds of learners.
- The ability to work collaboratively.
- One's best work.

Suggestions for Success

Here are some ideas for a successful interview portfolio:

- Balance the collection of artifacts so that all six NAEYC standards have approximately the same number of artifacts. For the showcase portfolio, three to five artifacts per standard are recommended.
- Choose only your very best work.
- Lead each section with your strongest artifacts.
- Use high-quality paper that has a professional look.
- Be consistent in style, type, and paper.
- Strive for a visual identity.
- Select recent and relevant examples.
- Include student work samples, especially with lesson plans and assessments.
- Use only clean copies.
- Put each page of the artifact in clear plastic sheet protectors.
- Use a variety of artifacts.
- Vary the reflective narratives.
- Include samples of technological competence throughout.
- Strive for neatness and careful organization.
- Spell-check and proofread everything.

Reevaluating Artifacts and Narratives

Once you have collected an adequate number of artifacts, it is time to evaluate each one thoughtfully to make sure it best exemplifies the NAEYC and InTASC standard where it is placed. While there is no definitive number of artifacts required, we recommend that you have a balanced number of artifacts in each of the six NAEYC standards, probably three, four, or five per standard.

Examine the portfolio assessment rating sheet in (Figure 9-1), the portfolio assessment tools (Figures 7-2, 7-3, and 7-5) in Chapter 7, or one provided by your college or university. Each of the six NAEYC or ten InTASC standards represents the overall objective of the standard, and the explanations in the second column represent the indicator(s) for that standard. Critically evaluate your artifacts and ask yourself, "Do the artifacts I have selected address each one of the indicators?" For example, under NAEYC Standard 4: Using Developmentally Effective Approaches to Connect with Children and Families, let's say that you have included four artifacts. But did you include an artifact and an accompanying reflective narrative that demonstrates that you support and expand learning through communication (Indicator 1)? Did you use appropriate strategies and resources to adapt learning to the needs of individual students (Indicator 2)? Did you integrate technology to engage students (Indicator 3)? Did one of your artifacts show how you respect families and how you worked collaboratively with them to meet specific goals (Indicator 4)? It's important to meet each indicator as well as the overall objective (standard).

As you review your selections, you may need to add new artifacts or refine your reflective narratives to address each indicator directly. Working with an evaluation tool will improve your understanding of the standards. By reshaping individual artifacts to better fit the indicators under each NAEYC or InTASC standard, you clarify your own understanding. Self-evaluate and reevaluate your work to date. Decide whether you need to add or delete artifacts, if you need to move artifacts from one standard to another, or if you have reflective narratives that need fine-tuning. Do your artifacts demonstrate your understanding of teaching young children and substantiate the educational principles of your particular academic institution?

Preparing for Your Portfolio Review

You can prepare for your portfolio interview in many ways, but we recommend peer evaluations, conferencing with your university instructor(s), mock interviews, and familiarity with your final professional portfolio. Once again, this involves ongoing reflection and analysis. Your portfolio is a working document. The more time you spend preparing for the portfolio evaluation, the more comfortable you will become with the NAEYC and InTASC standards and your artifacts. You will also need to be able to articulate how well your individual artifacts demonstrate your understanding of teaching young children and working with families, as well as the educational standards used by your particular academic institution.

Reviewing Prior to Your Defense

Ask your classmates, university supervisors, mentor-teachers, and instructors to review your portfolio and provide you with feedback. If you struggle with written expression, grammar, and spelling, ask a classmate, family member, or friend to check it for you. Use spell and grammar check on your computer. You may have a thoughtful, complete portfolio, but if it is full of errors, the errors are what assessors will focus on. Then the question is raised, "Is this preservice intern ready to take on the responsibility of teaching in an early childhood setting in a professional way?" Your portfolio is the tangible representation of you as a preservice teacher.

Throughout our program, some instructors do peer reviews as an in-class activity learning tool. Having the opportunity to look at others' portfolios can help you with your own portfolio. Your classmates may have included artifacts in their portfolios that you had not even considered using; they may have placed artifacts under NAEYC and InTASC standards that you had not contemplated. Look at and evaluate as many portfolios as you possibly can because you will grow and learn from each experience. Some instructors periodically grade and give constructive criticism on portfolio progress at various stages. These educational professionals can provide you with practical suggestions and guidance. This is also an opportunity for you to "strut your stuff" because a well-thought-out and organized portfolio clearly exemplifies your professional attributes.

Portfolio Defense

Prior to the portfolio review procedures used by your college or university, set up a mock portfolio interview as a practice session. For the practice mock interview, have one classmate sit on one side of the table with his or her portfolio and have additional classmates play the role of assessors. Allow time for the intern to present an introductory statement, and then have the assessment "panel" ask questions of the intern from a list provided. Permit enough time for all class members to practice the interviewee position. Practicing the presentation itself may help you to prepare for the actual interview and will provide you with questions that may arise during the actual portfolio review. Many of the questions asked may be similar to those you encounter when you interview for actual teaching positions. This practice talking about your assets as an educator may prove invaluable.

Figure 9-2 provides a list of sample interview questions. Know the "hot topics." In this era of strong accountability, be sure to be prepared for topics like using data to monitor instruction, using technology in the classroom, differentiating instruction, and classroom management.

- What is your philosophy of education?
- What artifact best represents you?
- How does your portfolio support your growth as a teacher?
- Describe how you incorporated NAEYC standards into your teaching.
- When you plan for instruction during a cycle of learning or a unit of learning, how do you know the students in your class achieved or accomplished the learning objective(s)? Include data to document each student's progress.
- What artifact in your portfolio best chronicles your growth as an early childhood educator? Show an example.
- Describe a particular lesson that includes cultural sensitivity and/or diversifies instruction so that all learners are successful. How does your evidence demonstrate that you facilitate learning for every individual student?
- How do effective classroom management strategies enhance instruction and student achievement? What strategies have you implemented and found to be effective? Present examples.
- How do you build a classroom community?
- How would you use technology in the classroom?
- How would you integrate multiple subjects so that students see the connections among all curricular areas?
- How do you encourage family involvement?
- Describe your planning process for a major project or unit.
- Describe your ideal lesson.
- Describe your teaching style. What could a visitor to your class expect to see?
- How do your assignments to students allow them the opportunity to express their creativity and individuality?
- Discuss and show an example of a thematic unit or a five-day cycle of learning.
- What was the "worst" lesson you ever taught? What did you learn from it?
- How do you incorporate diversity in your teaching? Provide evidence.
- How do you differentiate instruction? Present an example.
- What is a classroom management plan that you would incorporate in your classroom? Why?
- What role do standards play in your classroom?
- How do you modify your teaching to reach students who are struggling to perform at grade level? Provide illustrations or examples.
- How does data drive instruction in your classroom?
- Talk about and show examples of how you use assessment in your classroom.

FIGURE 9-2 *Sample Interview Questions*

The Presentation

The night of your presentation has come! You are excited but nervous. As you approach the assessors, take a deep breath. At our institution, the assessment panel is comprised of one university faculty member and one or two other educational professionals, often mentor-teachers or administrators from our professional development schools. All are dedicated persons with a strong understanding of our departmental standards and procedures and of the InTASC and NAEYC standards. They understand the skills, attributes, and dispositions of an early childhood professional.

Remember, the best portfolio in the world won't help you if you don't know how to use it. Let it help you respond to the assessors' questions. If an assessor asks you for an example of a time when a certain skill failed you, do not stress out. No one expects you to be perfect, but the assessors may want to see how you handle yourself. Give an example, but be sure to point out what you learned from the experience and how you would handle the situation now.

Suggestions for a Successful Presentation

- *Know your portfolio!* Consider making a copy of your table of contents so that during the portfolio review, you have a quick reference to the location of artifacts in your portfolio. Use your artifacts to support your verbal response to questions.
- *Know your audience.* Be knowledgeable about current "hot" issues in education and be able to articulate nonbiased, research-based understandings.
- *Dress for success.* Consider this a job interview and dress for the part. Wear clothing that is professional, relatively conservative, and comfortable.
- *Start off on the right foot.* Practice a firm handshake and making eye contact, and have a brief planned introductory statement to avoid an awkward silence.
- *Answer the question.* Try to provide a direct, concise answer to a direct question and use the artifacts of your portfolio as tangible support. Allow the portfolio assessors time to ask the necessary questions.

ACTIVITY 9-1

Choose your best artifacts that showcase your professional growth and learning.

Summary

A showcase portfolio "is compiled for the expressed purpose of giving others an effective and easy-to-read portrait of your professional competence" (Campbell et al., 2011, p. 4). When you present this work as a summative evaluation prior to graduation, you demonstrate the nature and quality of your day-to-day work. This evidence goes far beyond what words on a resume do. It sets you apart as a unique individual whose work depicts the knowledge, skills, dispositions, and attitudes necessary to succeed as a teacher of young children.

You have prepared for this event. Your careful thought in developing your showcase portfolio has demanded your time, energy, and meticulous reflection. You know your portfolio better than anyone; therefore, your presentation will be unique because it reflects your abilities, strengths, creativity, and professionalism. Confidence is the key to making a good impression. Know yourself. Present your achievements succinctly. Use your portfolio to provide concrete examples that clearly demonstrate your skills and your strengths. Good luck!

Suggested Website

www.towson.edu/idis/Pdf/PortfolioPrep.pdf

References

Campbell, D. M., Cignetti, P. B., Melenyzer, B. J., Nettles, D. H., & Wyman, R. M. (2011). *How to develop a professional portfolio: A manual for teachers* (5th ed.). Upper Saddle River, NJ: Pearson

Costantino, P. M., & DeLorenzo, M. N. (2009). *Developing a professional teaching portfolio: A guide for success* (3rd ed.). New York: Pearson.

Martin-Kniep, G. O. (1999). *Capturing the wisdom of practice: Professional portfolios*

Alexandria, VA.: Association of Supervision and Curriculum Development.

chapter 10

Taking Your Portfolio to the Next Step

So far, you have learned that the purpose of the portfolio is to document your professional growth and competence in the complex act of teaching through an organized collection of artifacts. The collection of these artifacts begins when you enter college and continues throughout your entire early childhood education program. Course assignments such as writing and implementing lesson plans, planning field trips, implementing service learning projects, engaging in action research, and participating in school improvement teams add value to teacher preparation, and they also often serve as viable artifacts. But what happens now? In this final chapter, we look at how your portfolio has prepared you to interview for potential teaching positions and enter the workforce as a professional in the field of early childhood education.

Preparation before the Interview

Keys to successful interviewing include knowing yourself—your strengths and weaknesses—and learning as much about the school system, the school, and the requirements of the job as you can. Present yourself as someone who has something to offer this particular school system or school. Arrive at the interview early. Dress appropriately and bring an interview portfolio with you so that you will be able to provide concrete examples that demonstrate your skills, knowledge, and attitudes related to teaching. Get a good night's sleep so that you are well rested and alert. Practice answering questions that you think will be asked by the interviewer or interview team.

The Interview Portfolio

Your interview portfolio is the probably the most important marketing tool you will ever create. Take the time and effort necessary to develop one that represents you. Use your showcase portfolio or any other artifacts that you have saved to prepare a portfolio specifically designed for a particular interview. For example, let's say that you are applying for a kindergarten position at your desired school. Put together personal documents that include a letter of introduction, a resume, university transcripts, Praxis I and II scores, a philosophy statement, and one or two letters of recommendation. Then include several artifacts that were specifically planned for kindergarten children. These artifacts could include, but are not limited to, lesson plans, work samples, and appropriate assessments. A wise choice would be to include a lesson plan with a reflection about your teaching effectiveness, documentation of student learning, and data to support both. Perhaps you want to include a lesson where you adapted instruction to meet the needs of all students. Select the best and most relevant of the documents.

The interviewer wants to gather as much relevant information about you as he or she can to assess how well your qualifications match the requirements of the position. When you have a portfolio with you, the interviewer can determine how well your portfolio artifacts relate to his or her needs (Kimeldorf, 1997). Sometimes interns complain that the interviewer "never looked at my portfolio." If you bring a busy principal a 3-inch binder with 30 artifacts, many times he or she could not possibly look at it carefully. Be wise. Be brief. Do not bring a massive portfolio with you to interviews. Your final interview portfolio probably should not exceed 25 pages, and shorter is better (Kimeldorf, 1997). Be highly selective and include only the most essential documents relevant to the position for which you are applying. If you are using an e-portfolio, be sure to let the interviewer know ahead of time that you will need access to a computer. If it is a web-based portfolio, you may also consider emailing the link to your interviewer before your interview. If your portfolio is saved to a flash drive or other portable data device, check it in advance to make sure that the documents that you need are easily accessible.

An interview portfolio is an asset. Some candidates create a small version of their portfolio that can be left with the interviewer. This can be a copied version that includes a small sampling of documents. Other interviewees develop a brochure that provides interviewers with a "portfolio at a glance" (Campbell et al., 2011, p. 99). Electronic portfolios can be copied onto DVDs and left with the interviewing team.

As you interview for jobs, remember that employers are looking for qualities and attributes in addition to teaching and learning competencies. Here are some you may want to consider:

- Ability to interact with others
- Ability to solve problems
- Ability to work with others as a team
- Appearance, dress, and grooming
- Communication skills
- Leadership potential
- Mature behavior and judgment
- Personal enthusiasm, poise, flexibility and a sense of humor
- Realistic appraisal of self and self-reflection
- Self-confidence
- Readiness to ask several good questions of your interviewer and perspective employer
- Work ethic/professional ethical standards (http://careers.d.umn.edu/cs_handbook/cshandbook_interviewing.html)

Figures 10-1, 10-2, and 10-3 are questions from one Maryland elementary school employer. These are the questions the administrators and grade-level teams ask of all interviewees for Head Start, kindergarten, and primary-grade applicants, respectively. Note that these questions are quite similar to the ones asked at your portfolio review.

| | / | / | / |
| Applicant Name and Employee ID | Position Interviewing For | Daytime Phone | Evening Phone |

1. Could we please see your resume?

2. Tell us about yourself and your background. Why would you want to teach a full-day Head Start class?

3. Talk about reading in preschool.

4. Talk about math in preschool.

5. Talk about your use of data and how you monitor student progress.

6. We have one other full-day Head Start class and two half-day pre-K classes. Talk about your collaboration with those staff members and other members of the staff.

7. How will you invite parents into your classroom and make them part of your program?

8. Do you have any questions for the panel?

COMMENTS:

FIGURE 10-1 *Head Start Teacher Interview Form*

| Applicant Name and Employee ID | Position Interviewing For | Daytime Phone | Evening Phone |

1. Could we please see your resume?

2. Tell us about yourself and your professional experiences.

3. How would your training, beliefs and professional experiences benefit a school with a diverse student body? (Standard I)

4. Are you familiar with the curriculum guides? Share an example of a lesson you taught from the guide. (Standard II)

5. Think of one of your best lessons. Tell us how you differentiated your instruction to meet the needs of all students. Please provide an example. (Standards I and II)

6. Describe the basic components of an effective reading program. If we came into your classroom during your reading block, what would we see? How do you ensure that all students achieve? (Standard II) (Same question using math as the content area.)

7. What techniques would you use for behavior management? Describe your discipline philosophy, with examples. (Standard III)

8. What strategies do you use to assess your students and how do you use these results to set measurable goals for your students? (Standard IV)

9. Describe how you collaborate with colleagues to plan for and identify the instructional needs of students. (Standard V)

10. Do you have any questions for the panel?

COMMENTS:

FIGURE 10-2 *Kindergarten Teacher Interview Form*

_____ / _____ / _____ / _____

Applicant Name   **Position Interviewing For**   **Daytime Phone**   **Evening Phone**
and Employee ID

1. Could we please see your resume?

2. Tell us about yourself and your professional experiences.

3. We have a diverse student population. How would your training, beliefs, and professional experiences benefit our students? (Standard I)

4. Think of one of your best lessons. Tell us how you differentiated your instruction to meet the needs of all students. Please provide an example. (Standards I and II)

5. Explain what we would see in a typical reading/math block. (Standard II)

6. Describe your discipline philosophy and what techniques you would use for behavior management. (Standard III)

7. What do you use to assess your students and how do you use the results to set measurable goals for them? (Standard IV)

8. Describe how you work with colleagues to meet the needs of your students. (Standard V)

9. Do you have any questions for us?

COMMENTS:

FIGURE 10-3 _Primary-Grade Teacher Interview Form_

The standards listed in parentheses in two of the interview forms (Figures 10-1, 10-2 and 10-3) are from the Montgomery County public schools in Maryland and are defined in later in the chapter.

Your New Role as Teacher in a Contemporary Society

As interns move from being students to being teachers, we wonder how the development of a portfolio, in all its forms, helps them understand the role of a teacher in a complex, challenging, and dynamic world. This became a question on a questionnaire that we asked a number of our interns to see if they felt that developing a portfolio was worth the time and effort it took. The questionnaire (see Figure 10-4) is given regularly to interns at varying intervals in the program, to administrators, and to mentor-teachers. The questionnaire can be used to determine how the portfolio demonstrates professional growth. Miguel, an intern, felt that using the NAEYC and InTASC standards helped him to think more clearly about each principle and what it meant. "Teaching as a profession is not just what a teacher does in the classroom, but [also] includes what a person does outside the classroom." He felt the portfolio process "illustrates the importance of having a well-rounded education." Alexandra, also an intern, noted that each NAEYC standard corresponded to an area where teachers need to be proficient in order to develop successful students.

Most students felt that the portfolio process, although time consuming, was important for three main reasons: (1) writing lesson plans, (2) assessment, and (3) reflection. Learning to write explicit, detailed lesson plans helped them meet the needs of all students.

---

1. How did the portfolio process help you to understand the role of a teacher in contemporary society?

2. How was your learning in professional courses demonstrated through the process of creating a portfolio?

3. How did the insertion of new artifacts each semester demonstrate your proficiency of the InTASC standards?

4. How did the portfolio process help you accept more responsibility for professional growth?

5. What was the strongest standard demonstrated in your portfolio?

6. What standard needed to be more developed in your portfolio?

7. How did the portfolio process demonstrate your professional growth?

8. Was the portfolio useful after your portfolio interview or during student teaching?

9. How did the reflective narrative help you connect theory to practice? Did this process help you grow as a teacher?

10. How could your experience through this process be improved?

Additional Comments:

FIGURE 10-4 *Questionnaire for Interns and Teachers*

Second, continuous attention to assessment was modeled in education classes as a process that occurred throughout the preservice teachers' university career. The concentration on portfolio development throughout the two- or four-year program helped interns understand that assessment is ongoing. For example, in most lessons, interns were required to assess students before, during, and after instruction; they understood that "process over product" has significant value. Learning to think is not a linear activity.

Third, the value of reflection was seen as significant for preservice teachers. Writing clear, reflective narratives forced them to relate their course assignments and practical field experiences to the standards that all beginning teachers should be able to exhibit. As one student noted, "The reflective narratives are the largest indicators of my understanding of the content in my courses."

How Did the Portfolio Process Demonstrate Your Professional Growth?

In answer to the question, "How did the portfolio process demonstrate your professional growth?" every student discussed change. Most students found the process gratifying, not frustrating (for example, "I enjoyed seeing how I grew as a professional"). Most students admitted that demonstrating professional growth got easier as they progressed in the program:

> "By the time I got to the student teaching semester, I was more familiar with the standards and curriculum."
>
> "My portfolio completely changed from freshman year until now. I've taken out all but one or two of the original artifacts."
>
> "I've learned to take responsibility for my own professional growth because the portfolio is the showcase of all my work. It is important to be able to support what I have included."
>
> "I was amused to see some the artifacts that I had included from the beginning of my college experience showed how much more I know now than I when I began."
>
> "I am able to look at what I have accomplished as an undergrad; learning to be a teacher is [documented] on paper."
>
> "This process has helped me get organized!"
>
> "The process ensures that we, as students, keep the standards in mind when completing assignments."
>
> "Since the NAEYC standards outline the qualities of effective early childhood teachers, this process helps me keep that goal in mind."

Now You Are a Professional

You have graduated. You have applied for, interviewed, and gotten a job. Now what? Can you use the portfolio to explore new opportunities and direct the path of your professional growth? Your portfolio, organized around a set of standards in your field, has helped you engage in the process of self-reflection and self-assessment. As you set new professional goals, the skills you have learned during the portfolio process will enhance your teaching and will help you plan for professional advancement (Campbell et al., 2011).

As an undergraduate, you probably completed an action research project. Now that you have your own classroom, you could research a variety of topics of interest to you. Such an undertaking might function as part of your school improvement plan (SIP) or as a collaborative project with team members. You might even want to publish your action research project in a professional journal or present it at a local workshop or a state or national conference. Your school or school system may encourage you to design your own professional development plan. Perhaps you are interested in service learning and engaging your class in a project that will benefit the school or the community. You may want to attend graduate school or begin the process for National Board Certification. All of these are ideas for professional development that could be documented in your professional teaching portfolio because "portfolios are . . . recognized as tools for supporting teacher evaluation, rewarding outstanding practice, issuing permanent certification, . . . awarding advancements, and certifying practitioners" (Campbell et al., 2011, p. 81). Documentation of your successes and your struggles is a valuable part of your continuing professional development.

As a new teacher, it is now your responsibility to demonstrate teaching competence using the standards developed and approved by your local school system or states. For example, the Montgomery County Public Schools school district in Maryland lists six standards in its *Professional Growth System Handbook*. These six performance standards are defined and supported by performance criteria (see Figure 10-5 and refer to http://www.nbpts.org). Examples of what a teacher can do to meet each standard are also provided in the county's handbook. These performance standards will not be new to a teacher who has been through the portfolio process in college because the performance standards are similar to the standards he or she used as a student. Under each standard in the handbook are performance criteria and examples of evidence of knowledge, planning skills, and successful instruction. A district-driven portfolio is a collection of items the teacher selects to demonstrate his or her competence as a teacher.

In addition to district standards, a number of states are developing performance-based processes for awarding continuing licenses to beginning teachers. A statewide product portfolio is a collection of evidence prescribed by the agency that will assess it. For example, required evidence could consist of videos, consecutive lesson plans, assessment measures, and student work samples that document growth (Bullock & Hawk, 2010).

Standard I: Teachers are committed to students and their learning.

Standard II: Teachers know the subjects they teach and how to teach those subjects to students.

Standard III: Teachers are responsible for establishing and managing student learning in a positive learning environment.

Standard IV: Teachers continually assess student progress, analyze the results, and adapt instruction to improve student achievement.

Standard V: Teachers are committed to continuous improvement and professional development.

Standard VI: Teachers exhibit a high degree of professionalism.

FIGURE 10-5 *School District Performance Standards*
Source: *http://montgomeryschoolsmd.org/departments/development/teams/admin/pgs_documents*

At the national level, the National Board for Professional Teaching Standards (NBPTS) provides voluntary advanced certification for the most experienced and accomplished teachers. In a policy statement updated in August 2002, NBPTS outlines what teachers should know and be able to do (National Board for Professional Teaching Standards, 2002, August). This policy outlines five core propositions that frame the knowledge, skills, dispositions, and beliefs that characterize exceptional teaching. The Early Childhood Generalist NBPTS Standards are now in their second edition (National Board for Professional Teaching Standards, 2001). Guided by nine standards outlined briefly in Figure 10-6, the assessment process is captured in

---

I. Understanding Young Children
Accomplished early childhood teachers use their knowledge of child development and their relationships with children and families to understand children as individuals and to plan in response to their unique needs and potentials.

II. Equity, Fairness, and Diversity
Accomplished early childhood teachers model and teach behaviors appropriate in a diverse society by creating a safe, secure learning environment for all children; by showing appreciation of and respect for the individual differences and unique needs of each member of the learning community; and by empowering children to treat others with, and to expect from others, equity, fairness, and dignity.

III. Assessment
Accomplished early childhood teachers recognize the strengths and weaknesses of multiple assessment methodologies and know how to use them effectively. Employing a variety of methods, they systematically observe, monitor, and document children's activities and behavior, analyzing, communicating, and using the information they glean to improve their work with children, parents, and others.

IV. Promoting Child Development and Learning
Accomplished early childhood teachers promote children's cognitive, social, emotional, physical, and linguistic development by organizing and orchestrating the environment in ways that best facilitate the development and learning of young children.

V. Knowledge of Integrated Curriculum
On the basis of their knowledge of how young children learn, of academic subjects, and of assessment, accomplished early childhood teachers design and implement developmentally appropriate learning experiences that integrate within and across the disciplines.

VI. Multiple Teaching Strategies for Meaningful Learning
Accomplished early childhood teachers use a variety of practices and resources to promote individual development, meaningful learning, and social cooperation.

VII. Family and Community Partnerships
Accomplished early childhood teachers work with and through families and communities to support children's learning and development.

VIII. Professional Partnerships
Accomplished early childhood teachers work as leaders and collaborators in the professional community to improve programs and practices for young children and their families.

IX. Reflective Practice
Accomplished early childhood teachers regularly analyze, evaluate, and synthesize to strengthen the quality and effectiveness of their work.

FIGURE 10-6 NBPTS *Early Childhood Generalist Standards* (2001)
Source: Printed with permission from The National Board for Professional Teaching Standards.

a portfolio that showcases your teaching practice using video recordings of interactions between you and your students, examples of key lesson components, explanations about the effectiveness of your practice, analysis of student responses to your teaching, in-depth written reflections on your teaching practices, evidence of your accomplishments outside the classroom that affects student learning, and documentation of your development as a learner and collaborator with families and communities (http://www.nbpts.org; Campbell et al., 2011). Elaboration on each standard discusses the knowledge, skills, dispositions, and habits of mind that describe accomplished teaching in the field (http://www.nbpts.org).

Summary

Students in early childhood education are trained in the important process of reflecting and documenting their growth over time. They are prepared to be insightful about their own teaching and learning.

As you move from your studies as an undergraduate to working as a professional, you carry the skills learned throughout the portfolio process to your classroom. You are able to articulate knowledge, dispositions, and attitudes to teach in diverse and culturally responsive classrooms. Not only was your portfolio an important benchmark in your undergraduate program, but it can remain a valuable tool throughout your professional career.

Reflection—the process by which teachers review instruction, think critically about pedagogy, and analyze the results to enhance or change their students' lives—is a critical component of the portfolio process and of teaching in today's world.

 ## Suggested Websites

Montgomery County Public Schools provides teacher evaluation performance standards, with descriptions, and examples of criteria for meeting each standard.

http://montgomeryshcollsmd.org/departments/development/teams/admin/pgs_documents

The National Board for Professional Teaching Standard provides standards, information, and applications for National Board Certification.

http://www.nbpts.org.

These websites prepare people looking for employment in education for interview questions and careers in education:

http://careers.d.umn.edu/cs_handbook/cshandbook_interviewing.html

www.career.vt.edu/Interviewing?TeachingInterviewQuestions.html

www.jobsearch.about.com/od/interviewquestionsanswers/a/teacherint.htm

www.teachingheart.net/teacherinterview.html

www.adprima.com/interview.htm

www.tips.atozteacherstuff.com/373/job-interviews

www.jobinterviewtools.com

www.teachingjobinterveiwsecrets.com

www.marquetteeducator.wordpress.com

References

Bullock, A. A., & Hawk, P. P. (2010). *Developing a teaching portfolio: A guide for preservice and practicing teachers* (3rd ed.). Upper Saddle River, NJ: Pearson Education.

Campbell, D. M., Cignetti, P. B., Melenyzer, B. J., Nettles, D. H., & Wyman, R. M. (2011). *How to develop a professional portfolio: A manual for teachers* (5th ed.). Upper Saddle River, NJ: Pearson Education.

Kimeldorf, M. (1997). *Portfolio power: The new way to showcase all your job skills and experiences.* Princeton, NJ: Peterson's Publishing Group.

National Board for Professional Teaching Standards. (2001). Early childhood generalist standards. Retrieved from www.nbpts.org

National Board for Professional Teaching Standards. (2002, August). What teachers should know and be able to do. Retrieved from www.nbpts.org

appendix A

· ·

Position Statement

NAEYC Standards for Early Childhood Professional Preparation Programs

NAEYC Standards for Early Childhood Professional Preparation Programs

**Position Statement Approved by the
NAEYC Governing Board July 2009**

A position statement of the National Asssociation for the Education of Young Children

Introduction

The purpose of this position statement

NAEYC Standards for Early Childhood Professional Preparation Programs represents a sustained vision for the early childhood field and more specifically for the programs that prepare the professionals working in the field. This 2009 revision of the standards is responsive to new knowledge, research and conditions while holding true to core values and principles of the founders of the profession. It is designed for use in a variety of ways by different sectors of the field while also supporting specific and critical policy structures, including state and national early childhood teacher credentialing, national accreditation of professional early childhood preparation programs, state approval of early childhood teacher education programs, and articulation agreements between various levels and types of professional development programs.

History

NAEYC has a long-standing commitment to the development and support of strong early childhood degree programs in institutions of higher education. NAEYC standard setting for degree programs in institutions of higher education began more than 25 years ago. This document is the third revision to NAEYC's Early Childhood Teacher Education Guidelines for Four- and Five-Year Programs (1982) and Guidelines for Early Childhood Education Programs in Associate Degree Granting Institutions (1985).

Development and publication of those first standards documents was made possible through the contributions of family and friends of Rose H. Alschuler, a founding member and first Secretary-Treasurer of NAEYC from 1929–1931. During the 1920s, Ms. Alschuler was an early proponent and director of the first public nursery schools in the United States. During the 1930s she directed Works Progress Administration (WPA) public nursery schools in Chicago. During World War II she chaired the National Commission for Young Children. Her life and legacy continue today as our field furthers its work to improve both programs for young children and programs that prepare early childhood professionals.

Standards Summary

Standard 1. Promoting Child Development and Learning

Students prepared in early childhood degree programs are grounded in a child development knowledge base. They use their understanding of young children's characteristics and needs and of the multiple interacting influences on children's development and learning to create environments that are healthy, respectful, supportive, and challenging for each child.

Key elements of Standard 1

1a: Knowing and understanding young children's characteristics and needs

1b: Knowing and understanding the multiple influences on development and learning

1c: Using developmental knowledge to create healthy, respectful, supportive, and challenging learning environments

Supporting explanation

The early childhood field has historically been grounded in a child development knowledge base, and early childhood programs have aimed to support a broad range of positive developmental outcomes for all young children. Although the scope and emphasis of that knowledge base have changed over the years and while early childhood professionals recognize that other sources of knowledge are also important influences on curriculum and programs for young children, early childhood practice continues to be deeply linked with a "sympathetic understanding of the young child" (Elkind 1994).

Well-prepared early childhood degree candidates base their practice on sound **knowledge and understanding of young children's characteristics and needs.** This foundation encompasses multiple, interrelated areas of children's development and learning—including physical, cognitive, social, emotional, language, and aesthetic domains; play, activity, and learning processes; and motivation to learn—and is supported by coherent theoretical perspectives and by current research.

Candidates also understand and apply their understanding of the **multiple influences on young children's development and learning** and

of how those influences may interact to affect development in both positive and negative ways. Those influences include the cultural and linguistic contexts for development, children's close relationships with adults and peers, economic conditions of children and families, children's health status and disabilities, individual developmental variations and learning styles, opportunities to play and learn, technology and the media, and family and community characteristics. Candidates also understand the potential influence of early childhood programs, including early intervention, on short- and long-term outcomes for children.

Candidates' competence is demonstrated in their ability to **use developmental knowledge to create healthy, respectful, supportive, and challenging learning environments** for all young children (including curriculum, interactions, teaching practices, and learning materials). Such environments reflect *four critical features.*

- First, the environments are *healthy*—that is, candidates possess the knowledge and skills needed to promote young children's physical and psychological health, safety, and sense of security.

- Second, the environments reflect *respect* for each child as a feeling, thinking individual and then for each child's culture, home language, individual abilities or disabilities, family context, and community. In respectful environments, candidates model and affirm antibias perspectives on development and learning.

- Third, the learning environments created by early childhood teacher candidates are supportive. Candidates demonstrate their belief in young children's ability to learn, and they show that they can use their understanding of early childhood development to help each child understand and make meaning from her or his experiences through play, spontaneous activity, and guided investigations.

- Finally, the learning environments that early childhood candidates create are appropriately *challenging*. In other words, candidates apply their knowledge of contemporary theory and research to construct learning environments that provide achievable and stretching experiences for all children—including children with special abilities and children with disabilities or developmental delays.

Standard 2. Building Family and Community Relationships

Students prepared in early childhood degree programs understand that successful early childhood education depends upon partnerships with children's families and communities. They know about, understand, and value the importance and complex characteristics of children's families and communities. They use this understanding to create respectful, reciprocal relationships that support and empower families and to involve all families in their children's development and learning.

Key elements of Standard 2

2a: Knowing about and understanding diverse family and community characteristics

2b: Supporting and engaging families and communities through respectful, reciprocal relationships

2c: Involving families and communities in their children's development and learning

Supporting explanation

Because young children's lives are so embedded in their families and communities and research indicates that successful early childhood education depends upon partnerships with families and communities, early childhood professionals need to thoroughly understand and apply their knowledge in this area.

First, well-prepared candidates possess **knowledge and understanding of diverse family and community characteristics** and of the many influences on families and communities. Family theory and research provide a knowledge base. Socioeconomic conditions; family structures, relationships, stresses, and supports (including the impact of having a child with special needs); home language; cultural values; ethnicity; community resources, cohesiveness, and organization—knowledge of these and other factors creates a deeper understanding of young children's lives. This knowledge is critical to the candidates' ability to help children learn and develop well.

Second, candidates possess the knowledge and skills needed to **support and engage diverse families through respectful, reciprocal relationships.** Candidates understand how to build posi-

tive relationships, taking families' preferences and goals into account and incorporating knowledge of families' languages and cultures. Candidates demonstrate respect for variations across cultures in family strengths, expectations, values, and childrearing practices. Candidates consider family members to be resources for insight into their children, as well as resources for curriculum and program development. Candidates know about and demonstrate a variety of communication skills to foster such relationships, emphasizing informal conversations while also including appropriate uses of conferencing and technology to share children's work and to communicate with families.

In their work, early childhood teacher candidates develop cultural competence as they build relationships with diverse families, including those whose children have disabilities or special characteristics or learning needs; families who are facing multiple challenges in their lives; and families whose languages and cultures may differ from those of the early childhood professional. Candidates also understand that their relationships with families include assisting families in finding needed resources, such as mental health services, health care, adult education, English language instruction, and economic assistance that may contribute directly or indirectly to their children's positive development and learning. Well-prepared early childhood candidates are able to identify such resources and know how to connect families with appropriate services, including help with planning transitions from one educational or service system to another.

Finally, well-prepared candidates possess essential skills to **involve families and communities in many aspects of children's development and learning.** They understand and value the role of parents and other important family members as children's primary teachers. Candidates understand how to go beyond parent conferences to engage families in curriculum planning, assessing children's learning, and planning for children's transitions to new programs. When their approaches to family involvement are not effective, candidates evaluate and modify those approaches rather than assuming that families "are just not interested."

Standard 3. Observing, Documenting, and Assessing to Support Young Children and Families

Students prepared in early childhood degree programs understand that child observation, documentation, and other forms of assessment are central to the practice of all early childhood professionals. They know about and understand the goals, benefits, and uses of assessment. They know about and use systematic observations, documentation, and other effective assessment strategies in a responsible way, in partnership with families and other professionals, to positively influence the development of every child.

Key elements of Standard 3

3a: Understanding the goals, benefits, and uses of assessment

3b: Knowing about and using observation, documentation, and other appropriate assessment tools and approaches

3c: Understanding and practicing responsible assessment to promote positive outcomes for each child

3d: Knowing about assessment partnerships with families and with professional colleagues

Supporting explanation

Although definitions vary, in these standards the term *assessment* includes all methods through which early childhood professionals gain understanding of children's development and learning. Ongoing, systematic observations and other informal and formal assessments are essential for candidates to appreciate children's unique qualities; to develop appropriate goals; and to plan, implement, and evaluate effective curriculum. Although assessment may take many forms, early childhood candidates demonstrate its central role by embedding assessment-related activities in curriculum and daily routines so that assessment becomes a habitual part of professional life.

Well-prepared early childhood candidates can explain the central **goals, benefits, and uses of assessment.** In considering the goals of assessment, candidates articulate and apply the concept of *alignment*—good assessment is consistent with and connected to appropriate goals, curriculum,

and teaching strategies for young children. The candidates know how to use assessment as a positive tool that supports children's development and learning and improves outcomes for young children and families. Candidates are able to explain positive uses of assessment and exemplify these in their own work, while also showing an awareness of the potentially negative uses of assessment in early childhood programs and policies.

Many aspects of effective assessment require collaboration with families and with other professionals. Through **partnerships with families and with professional colleagues**, candidates use positive assessment to identify the strengths of families and children. Through appropriate screening and referral, assessment may also result in identifying children who may benefit from special services. Both family members and, as appropriate, members of interprofessional teams may be involved in assessing children's development, strengths, and needs. As new practitioners, candidates may have had limited opportunities to experience such partnerships, but they demonstrate essential knowledge and core skills in team building and in communicating with families and colleagues from other disciplines.

Early childhood assessment includes **observation and documentation and other appropriate assessment strategies.** Effective teaching of young children begins with thoughtful, appreciative, systematic observation and documentation of each child's unique qualities, strengths, and needs. Observation gives insight into how young children develop and how they respond to opportunities and obstacles in their lives. Observing young children in classrooms, homes, and communities helps candidates develop a broad sense of who children are—as individuals, as group members, as family members, as members of cultural and linguistic communities. Candidates demonstrate skills in conducting systematic observations, interpreting those observations, and reflecting on their significance. Because spontaneous *play* is such a powerful window on all aspects of children's development, well-prepared candidates create opportunities to observe children in playful situations as well as in more formal learning contexts.

Many *young children with disabilities* are included in early childhood programs, and early identification of children with developmental delays or disabilities is very important. All beginning professionals, therefore, need essential knowledge about how to collect relevant information, including appropriate uses of screening tools and play-based assessments, not only for their own planning but also to share with families and with other professionals. Well-prepared candidates are able to choose valid tools that are developmentally, culturally, and linguistically appropriate; use the tools correctly; adapt tools as needed, using assistive technology as a resource; make appropriate referrals; and interpret assessment results, with the goal of obtaining valid, useful information to inform practice and decision making.

Although assessment can be a positive tool for early childhood professionals, it has also been used in inappropriate and harmful ways. Well-prepared candidates understand and practice **responsible assessment.** Candidates understand that responsible assessment is ethically grounded and guided by sound professional standards. It is collaborative and open. Responsible assessment supports children, rather than being used to exclude them or deny them services. Candidates demonstrate understanding of appropriate, responsible assessment practices for culturally and linguistically diverse children and for children with developmental delays, disabilities, or other special characteristics. Finally, candidates demonstrate knowledge of legal and ethical issues, current educational concerns and controversies, and appropriate practices in the assessment of diverse young children.

Standard 4. Using Developmentally Effective Approaches to Connect with Children and Families

Students prepared in early childhood degree programs understand that teaching and learning with young children is a complex enterprise, and its details vary depending on children's ages, characteristics, and the settings within which teaching and learning occur. They understand and use positive relationships and supportive interactions as the foundation for their work with young children and families. Students know, understand, and use a wide array of developmentally appropriate approaches, instructional strategies, and tools to connect with children and families and positively influence each child's development and learning.

Key elements of Standard 4

4a: Understanding positive relationships and supportive interactions as the foundation of their work with children

4b: Knowing and understanding effective strategies and tools for early education

4c: Using a broad repertoire of developmentally appropriate teaching/learning approaches

4d: Reflecting on their own practice to promote positive outcomes for each child

Supporting explanation

Early childhood candidates demonstrate that they understand the theories and research that support **the importance of relationships and high-quality interactions in early education**. In their practice, they display warm, nurturing interactions with each child, communicating genuine liking for and interest in young children's activities and characteristics. Throughout the years that children spend in early childhood settings, their successful learning is dependent not just on instruction but also on personal connections with important adults. Through these connections children develop not only academic skills but also positive learning dispositions and confidence in themselves as learners. Responsive teaching creates the conditions within which very young children can explore and learn about their world. The close attachments children develop with their teachers/caregivers, the expectations and beliefs that adults have about young children's capacities, and the warmth and responsiveness of adult-child interactions are powerful influences on positive developmental and educational outcomes. How children expect to be treated and how they treat others are significantly shaped in the early childhood setting. Candidates in early childhood programs develop the capacity to build a caring community of learners in the early childhood setting.

Early childhood professionals need **a broad repertoire of effective strategies and tools** to help young children learn and develop well. Candidates must ground their curriculum in a set of core approaches to teaching that are supported by research and are closely linked to the processes of early development and learning. In a sense, those approaches *are* the curriculum for infants and toddlers, although academic content can certainly be embedded in each of them. With preschool and early primary grade children, the relative weight and explicitness of subject matter or academic content become more evident in the curriculum, yet the core approaches or strategies remain as a consistent framework. Engaging conversations, thought-provoking questions, provision of materials, and spontaneous activities are all evident in the candidate's repertoire of teaching skills.

Candidates demonstrate the essential *dispositions* to develop positive, respectful relationships with children whose cultures and languages may differ from their own, as well as with children who may have developmental delays, disabilities, or other learning challenges. In making the transition from family to a group context, very young children need continuity between the practices of family members and those used by professionals in the early childhood setting. Their feelings of safety and confidence depend on that continuity. Candidates know the cultural practices and contexts of the young children they teach, and they adapt practices as they continue to develop *cultural competence*—culturally relevant knowledge and skills.

Well-prepared early childhood professionals make purposeful use of various learning formats based on their understanding of children as individuals and as part of a group, and on alignment with important educational and developmental goals. A flexible, research-based **repertoire of teaching/learning approaches to promote young children's development** includes

- Fostering oral language and communication
- Drawing from a continuum of teaching strategies
- Making the most of the environment, schedule, and routines
- Setting up all aspects of the indoor and outdoor environment
- Focusing on children's individual characteristics, needs, and interests
- Linking children's language and culture to the early childhood program
- Teaching through social interactions
- Creating support for play
- Addressing children's challenging behaviors
- Supporting learning through technology
- Using integrative approaches to curriculum

All of these teaching approaches are effective across the early childhood age span. From the infant/toddler room to the early grades, young children are developing not only early language and reading skills but also the *desire* to communicate, read, and write. They are developing not only early math and science skills and concepts but also the *motivation* to solve problems. They are developing empathy, sociability, friendships, self-concept, and self-esteem. Concept acquisition, reasoning, self-regulation, planning and organization, emotional understanding and empathy, sociability—development of all of these is deeply entwined with early experiences in mathematics, language, literacy, science, and social studies in the early education program.

Early childhood professionals make decisions about their practice based on expertise. They make professional judgments through each day based on knowledge of child development and learning, individual children, and the social and cultural contexts in which children live. From this knowledge base, effective teachers design activities, routines, interactions, and curriculum for specific children and groups of children. They consider both what to teach and how to teach, developing the habit of **reflective, responsive, and intentional practice** to promote positive outcomes for each child.

Standard 5. Using Content Knowledge to Build Meaningful Curriculum

Students prepared in early childhood degree programs use their knowledge of academic disciplines to design, implement, and evaluate experiences that promote positive development and learning for each and every young child. Students understand the importance of developmental domains and academic (or content) disciplines in an early childhood curriculum. They know the essential concepts, inquiry tools, and structure of content areas, including academic subjects, and can identify resources to deepen their understanding. Students use their own knowledge and other resources to design, implement, and evaluate meaningful, challenging curricula that promote comprehensive developmental and learning outcomes for every young child.

Key elements of Standard 5

5a: Understanding content knowledge and resources in academic disciplines

5b: Knowing and using the central concepts, inquiry tools, and structures of content areas or academic disciplines

5c: Using their own knowledge, appropriate early learning standards, and other resources to design, implement, and evaluate meaningful, challenging curricula for each child.

Supporting explanation

Strong, effective early childhood curricula do not come out of a box or a teacher-proof manual. Early childhood professionals have an especially challenging task in developing effective curricula. As suggested in Standard 1, well-prepared candidates ground their practice in a thorough, research-based understanding of young children's development and learning processes. In developing curriculum, they recognize that every child constructs knowledge in personally and culturally familiar ways. In addition, in order to make curriculum powerful and accessible to all, well-prepared candidates develop curriculum that is free of biases related to ethnicity, religion, gender, or ability status—and, in fact, the curriculum actively counters such biases.

The teacher of children from birth through age 8 must be well versed in **the essential content knowledge and resources in many academic disciplines**. Because children are encountering those content areas for the first time, early childhood professionals set the foundations for later understanding and success. Going beyond conveying isolated facts, well-prepared early childhood candidates possess the kind of content knowledge that focuses on the "big ideas," methods of investigation and expression, and organization of the major academic disciplines. Thus, the early childhood professional knows not only *what* is important in each content area but also *why* it is important— how it links with earlier and later understandings both within and across areas. Because of its central place in later academic competence, the domain of language and literacy requires in-depth, research-based understanding and skill. Mathematics too is increasingly recognized as an essential foundation.

Teachers of young children demonstrate the understanding of **central concepts, inquiry tools, and structure of content areas** needed to provide appropriate environments that support learning in each content area for all children, beginning in infancy (through foundational developmental experiences) and extending through the primary grades. Candidates demonstrate basic knowledge of the research base underlying each content area and of the core concepts and standards of professional organizations in each content area. They rely on sound resources for that knowledge. Finally, candidates demonstrate that they can analyze and critique early childhood curriculum experiences in terms of the relationship of the experiences to the research base and to professional standards.

Well-prepared candidates choose their approaches to the task depending on the ages and developmental levels of the children they teach. They use their own **knowledge, appropriate early learning standards, and other resources to design, implement, and evaluate meaningful, challenging curriculum for each child.** With the youngest children, early childhood candidates emphasize the key experiences that will support later academic skills and understandings—with reliance on the core approaches and strategies described in sub-standard 4b and with emphasis on oral language and the development of children's background knowledge. Working with somewhat older or more skilled children, candidates also identify those aspects of each subject area that are critical to children's later academic competence. With all children, early childhood professionals support later success by modeling engagement in challenging subject matter and by building children's faith in themselves as young learners— young mathematicians, scientists, artists, readers, writers, historians, economists, and geographers (although children may not think of themselves in such categories).

Early childhood curriculum content/discipline areas include learning goals, experiences, and assessment in the following academic disciplines or content areas:

- Language and literacy
- The arts—music, creative movement, dance, drama, and visual arts
- Mathematics

- Science
- Physical activity, physical education, health and safety
- Social studies

Designing, implementing, and evaluating meaningful, challenging curriculum requires alignment with appropriate early learning standards and knowledgeable use of the discipline's resources to focus on key experiences for each age group and each individual child.

Early childhood teacher candidates, just like experienced teachers, go beyond their own basic knowledge to identify and use high-quality resources, including books, standards documents, Web resources, and individuals who have specialized content expertise in developing early childhood curriculum. In addition to national or state standards (NAEYC & NAECS/SDE 2002), several larger goals are also held by all early childhood teachers:

- **Security and self-regulation.** Appropriate, effective curriculum creates a secure base from which young children can explore and tackle challenging problems. Well-implemented curriculum also helps children become better able to manage or regulate their expressions of emotion and, over time, to cope with frustration and manage impulses effectively rather than creating high levels of frustration and anxiety.

- **Problem-solving and thinking skills.** Candidates who have skills in developing and implementing meaningful, challenging curricula will also support young children's ability—and motivation—to solve problems and think well.

- **Academic and social competence.** Because good early childhood curriculum is aligned with young children's developmental and learning styles, it supports the growth of academic and social skills.

With these goals in mind, candidates develop curriculum to include both planned and spontaneous experiences that are developmentally appropriate, meaningful, and challenging for all young children, including those with developmental delays or disabilities; address cultural and linguistic diversities; lead to positive learning outcomes; and,as children become older, develop positive dispositions

toward learning within each content area.

Standard 6. Becoming a Professional

Students prepared in early childhood degree programs identify and conduct themselves as members of the early childhood profession. They know and use ethical guidelines and other professional standards related to early childhood practice. They are continuous, collaborative learners who demonstrate knowledgeable, reflective, and critical perspectives on their work, making informed decisions that integrate knowledge from a variety of sources. They are informed advocates for sound educational practices and policies.

Key elements of Standard 6

6a: Identifying and involving oneself with the early childhood field

6b: Knowing about and upholding ethical standards and other professional guidelines

6c: Engaging in continuous, collaborative learning to inform practice

6d: Integrating knowledgeable, reflective, and critical perspectives on early education

6e: Engaging in informed advocacy for children and the profession

The early childhood field has a distinctive history, values, knowledge base, and mission. Early childhood professionals, including beginning teachers, have a strong **identification and involvement with the early childhood field** to better serve young children and their families. Well-prepared candidates understand the nature of a profession. They know about the many connections between the early childhood field and other related disciplines and professions with which they may collaborate while serving diverse young children and families. Candidates are also aware of the broader contexts and challenges within which early childhood professionals work. They consider current issues and trends that might affect their work in the future.

Because young children are at such a critical point in their development and learning, and because they are vulnerable and cannot articulate their own rights and needs, early childhood professionals have compelling responsibilities to **know about and uphold ethical guidelines and other**

professional standards. The profession's code of ethical conduct guides the practice of responsible early childhood educators. Well-prepared candidates are very familiar with NAEYC's Code of Ethical Conduct and are guided by its ideals and principles. This means honoring their responsibilities to uphold high standards of confidentiality, sensitivity, and respect for children, families, and colleagues. Candidates know how to use the Code to analyze and resolve professional ethical dilemmas and are able to give defensible justifications for their resolutions of those dilemmas. Well-prepared candidates also know and obey relevant laws, such as those pertaining to child abuse, the rights of children with disabilities, and school attendance. Finally, candidates are familiar with relevant professional guidelines, such as national, state, or local standards for content and child outcomes; position statements about, for example, early learning standards, linguistic and cultural diversity, early childhood mathematics, technology in early childhood, prevention of child abuse, child care licensing requirements, and other professional standards affecting early childhood practice.

Continuous, collaborative learning to inform practice is a hallmark of a professional in any field. An attitude of inquiry is evident in well-prepared candidates' writing, discussion, and actions. Whether engaging in classroom-based research, investigating ways to improve their own practices, participating in conferences, or finding resources in libraries and on Internet sites, candidates demonstrate self-motivated, purposeful learning that directly influences the quality of their work with young children. Candidates—and professional preparation programs—view graduation or licensure not as the final demonstration of competence but as one milestone among many, including professional development experiences before and beyond successful degree completion.

At its most powerful, learning is socially constructed in interaction with others. Even as beginning teachers, early childhood candidates demonstrate involvement in collaborative learning communities with other candidates, higher education faculty, and experienced early childhood practitioners. By working together on common challenges, with lively exchanges of ideas, members of such communities benefit from one another's perspectives. Candidates also demonstrate understanding of and essential skills in interdisciplinary collaboration. Because many children with disabilities and other special needs are included in early childhood programs, every practitioner needs to understand the role of the other professionals who may be involved in young children's care and education (e.g., special educators, reading specialists, speech and hearing specialists, physical and occupational therapists, school psychologists). Candidates demonstrate that they have the essential communication skills and knowledge base to engage in interdisciplinary team meetings as informed partners and to fulfill their roles as part of Individualized Family Service Plan and Individualized Education Program (IFSP/IEP) teams for children with developmental delays or disabilities. They use technology effectively with children, with peers, and as a professional resource.

Well-prepared candidates' practice is influenced by **knowledgeable, reflective, and critical perspectives.** As professionals, early childhood candidates' decisions and advocacy efforts are grounded in multiple sources of knowledge and multiple perspectives. Even routine decisions about what materials to use for an activity, whether to intervene in a dispute between two children, how to organize nap time, what to say about curriculum in a newsletter, or what to tell families about new video games are informed by a professional context, research-based knowledge, and values. In their work with young children, candidates show that they make and justify decisions on the basis of their *knowledge* of the central issues, professional values and standards, and research findings in their field. They also show evidence of *reflective approaches* to their work, analyzing their own practices in a broader context, and using reflections to modify and improve their work with young children. Finally, well-prepared candidates display a *critical stance*, examining their own work, sources of professional knowledge, and the early childhood field with a questioning attitude. Their work demonstrates that they do not just accept a simplistic source of truth; instead, they recognize that while early childhood educators share the same core professional values, they do not agree on all of the field's central questions. Candidates demonstrate an understanding that through dialogue and attention to differences, early childhood professionals will continue to reach new levels of shared knowledge.

Finally, early childhood candidates demonstrate that they can engage in **informed advocacy for children and families and the profession.** They know about the central policy issues in the field, including professional compensation, financing of the early education system, and standards setting and assessment. They are aware of and engaged in examining ethical issues and societal concerns about program quality and provision of early childhood services and the implications of those issues for advocacy and policy change. Candidates have a basic understanding of how public policies are developed, and they demonstrate essential advocacy skills, including verbal and written communication and collaboration with others around common issues.

References

Introduction

AACC (American Association of Community Colleges). 2009a. AACC statement regarding the Project on Student Loan Debt report on community college loan access. www.aacc.nche.edu/About/Positions/Pages/ps04162008.aspx

AACC. 2009b. Fast facts. www.aacc.nche.edu/AboutCC/Pages/fastfacts.aspx

AACC. 1998. AACC position statement on the associate degree. www.aacc.nche.edu/About/Positions/Pages/ps08011998.aspx

Bogard, K., F. Traylor, & R. Takanishi. 2008. Teacher education and PK outcomes: Are we asking the right questions? *Early Childhood Research Quarterly* 23 (1): 1–6.

Burchinal, M., M. Hyson, & M. Zaslow. 2008. *Competencies and credentials for early childhood educators: What do we know and what do we need to know?* NHSA Dialog Briefs 11 (1).

Curenton, S. 2005. Toward better definition and measurement of early childhood professional development. In *Critical issues in early childhood* professional development, eds. M. Zaslow & I. Martinez-Beck, 17–19. Baltimore:. Brookes.

Darling-Hammond, L. 2007. We need to invest in math and science teachers. *The Chronicle Review* 54 (17): B20. http://chronicle.com/weekly/v54/i17/17b02001.htm

Early, D., & P. Winton. 2001. Preparing the workforce: early childhood teacher preparation at 2- and 4-year institutions of higher education. *Early Childhood Research Quarterly* 16 (3): 285–306.

Gilliam, W. S. 2008. *Implementing policies to reduce the likelihood of preschool expulsion.* Foundation for Child Development FCD Policy Brief 7. http://ziglercenter.yale.edu/documents/PreKExpulsionBrief2.pdf

Haynes, M., & J. Levin. 2009. *Promoting quality in preK–grade 3 classrooms: findings and results from NASBE's Early Childhood Education Network.* NASBE Issues in Brief. Arlington, VA: National Association of State Boards of Education.

Hyson, M., H.B. Tomlinson, & C.A.S. Morris. 2009. Quality improvement in early childhood teacher education faculty perspectives and recommendations for the future. *Early Childhood Research and Practice* 11 (1). http://ecrp.uiuc.edu/v11n1/hyson.html

Karp, N. 2005. Designing models for professional development at the local, state, and national levels. In *Critical issues in early childhood professional development*, eds. M. Zaslow & I. Martinez-Beck, 225–30. Baltimore: Brookes.

Kelly, P., & G. Camilli. 2007. *The impact of teacher education on outcomes in center-based early childhood education programs: A meta-analysis.* New Brunswick, NJ: National Institute for Early Education Research.

LeMoine, S. 2008 *Workforce designs: A policy blueprint for state early childhood professional development systems.* Washington, DC. NAEYC.

Lima, C., K.L. Maxwell, H. Able-Booneb, & C.R. Zimmer. 2009. Cultural and linguistic diversity in early childhood teacher preparation: The impact of contextual characteristics on coursework and practica. *Early Childhood Research Quarterly* 24 (1): 64–76.

Lutton, A.. 2009. NAEYC early childhood professional preparation standards: A vision for tomorrow's early childhood teachers. 2009. In *Conversations on early childhood teacher education: Voices from the Working Forum for Teacher Educators*, eds. A. Gibbons & C. Gibbs. Redmond, WA: World Forum Foundation and New Zealand Tertiary College.

Martinez-Beck, I., & M. Zaslow. 2005. Introduction: The context for critical issues in early childhood professional development. In *Critical issues in early childhood professional development*, eds. M. Zaslow & I. Martinez-Beck, 1-15. Baltimore: Brookes.

NAEYC & SRCD (Society for Research in Child Development). 2008. Using research to improve outcomes for young children: A call for action. Final report of the Wingspread Conference, September 18–20, 2007. *Early Childhood Research Quarterly* 23 (4): 591–96.

Ray, A.., B. Bowman, & J. Robbins. 2006. *Preparing early childhood teachers to successfully educate* all *children: The contribution of four-year undergraduate teacher preparation programs.* Report to the Foundation for Child Development on the Project on Race, Class, and Culture in Early Childhood. Chicago: Erikson Institute. www.erikson.edu/PageContent/en-us/Documents/pubs/Teachered.pdf

Snow, K.L. 2005. Completing the model: Connecting early child care worker professional development with child outcomes. In *Critical issues in early childhood professional development*, eds. M. Zaslow & I. Martinez-Beck, 137–140). Baltimore: Brookes.

Snyder, T.D., S.A. Dillow, & C.M. Hoffman. 2009. *Digest of education statistics 2008.* NCES #2009-020. Washington, DC: National Center for Education Statistics, Institute of Educational Sciences, U.S. Department of Education. http://nces.ed.gov/pubsearch/pubsinfo.asp?pubid=2009020

Tout, K., M. Zaslow, & D. Berry. 2005. Quality and qualifications: Links between professional development and quality in early care and education settings. In *Critical issues in early childhood professional development*, eds. M. Zaslow & I. Martinez-Beck, 77–110. Baltimore: Brookes.

Washington, V. 2008. *Role, relevance, reinvention: Higher education in the field of early care and education.* Boston: Wheelock College.

Whitebook, M., L. Sakai, F. Kipnis, M. Almaraz, E. Suarez, & D. Bellm. 2008. Learning together: A study of six B.A. completion cohort programs in early care and education. Year I Report. www.irle.berkeley.edu/cscce/pdf/learning_together08.pdf

Zaslow, M. 2005. Charting a course for improved professional development across varying programs and practices. In *Critical issues in early childhood professional development*, eds. M. Zaslow & I. Martinez-Beck, 351–53. Baltimore: Brookes.

Standard 1: Importance of Knowing Child Development

Bowman, B.T., S. Donovan, & M.S. Burns. 2000. *Eager to learn: Educating our preschoolers*. Washington, DC: National Academies Press. [1, 4]

Bronfenbrenner, U. 2004. *Making human beings human: Bioecological perspectives on human development*. Thousand Oaks, CA: Sage. [1]

Buysse, V., & P.W. Wesley. 2006. *Evidence-based practice in the early childhood field*. Washington, DC: Zero to Three Press. [1]

Copple, C., & S. Bredekamp, eds. 2009. *Developmentally appropriate practice in early childhood programs serving children from birth through age 8*. Washington, DC: NAEYC. [1, 4, 5]

Essa, E.L., M.M. & Burnham, eds.2009. *Informing our practice: Useful research on young children's development*. Washington, DC: NAEYC. [1,4]

Hendrick, J., & P. Weissman. 2009. *The whole child: Developmental education for the early years*. Upper Saddle River, NJ: Prentice Hall. [1]

National Research Council & Institute of Medicine. 2000 *From neurons to neighborhoods: The science of early childhood development*. Jack P. Shonkoff and Deborah A. Phillips, eds.; Committee on Integrating the Science of Early Childhood Development; Board on Children, Youth, and Families of the Commission on Behavioral and Social Sciences and Education. Washington, DC: National Academies Press. [1]

NCATE & NICHD (National Institute of Child Health and Human Development). 2006. *Child and adolescent development research and teacher education: Evidence-based pedagogy, policy, and practice*. Retrieved June 1, 2009 at www.ncate.org/documents/research/ChildAdolDevTeacherEd.pdf [1]

NICHD Early Child Care Research Network. 2005. *Child care and child development: Results from the NICHD Study of Early Child Care and Youth Development*. New York: Guilford. [1]

Rogoff, B. 2003. *The cultural nature of human development*. Oxford, UK: Oxford University Press. [1]

Tabors, P.O. 2008. One child, two languages: A guide for early childhood educators of children learning English as a second language. Baltimore, MD: Brookes. [1, 4]

Standard 2: Building Family and Community Relationships

Bouffard, S., & H. Weiss. 2008. Thinking big: A new framework for family involvement policy, practice, and research. *The Evaluation Exchange* 14 (1&2): 2–5. [2]

DEC (Division for Early Childhood) & NAEYC. 2008. Early childhood inclusion: Joint position statement of the Division for Early Childhood (DEC) and the National Association for the Education of Young Children (NAEYC). www.naeyc.org/about/positions/pdf/DEC_NAEYC_EC.pdf [2]

Epstein, J. 2001. *School, family, and community partnerships: Preparing educators and improving schools*. Boulder, CO: Westview. [2]

Epstein, J. L., & S.B. Sheldon. 2006. *Moving forward: Ideas for research on school, family, and community partnerships*. Retrieved June 1, 2009 at www.csos.jhu.edu/P2000/pdf/Literature%20Review%20-%20Epstein%20and%20Sheldon%2006.pdf [2]

Henderson, A.T., & K.L. Mapp. 2002. *A new wave of evidence: The impact of school, family, and community connections on student achievement*. Austin, TX: National Center for Family & Community Connections with Schools, Southwest Educational Development Laboratory. Retrieved June 1, 2009 at www.sedl.org/connections/resources/evidence.pdf [2]

Lopez, M.E., H. Kreider, & M. Caspe. 2004. Co-constructing family involvement. *Evaluation Exchange* X (4): 2–3. [2]

Lynch, E.W., & M.J. Hanson. 2004. *Developing cross-cultural competence: A guide for working with children and their families*. Baltimore, MD: Brookes. [2]

Ray, A.., B. Bowman, & J. Robbins. 2006. *Preparing early childhood teachers to successfully educate all children: The contribution of four-year undergraduate teacher preparation programs*. Report to the Foundation for Child Development on the Project on Race, Class, and Culture in Early Childhood. Chicago: Erikson Institute. www.erikson.edu/PageContent/en-us/Documents/pubs/Teachered.pdf

Valdés, G. 1999. *Con respeto: Bridging the distances between culturally diverse families and schools. An ethnographic portrait*. New York: Teachers College Press. [2]

Weiss, H.B., M. Caspe, & M.E. Lopez. 2006. *Family involvement in early childhood education*. Cambridge, MA: Harvard Family Research Project. [2]

Xu, Y., & J. Filler. 2008. Facilitating family involvement and support for inclusive education. *The School Community Journal* 18 (2): 53–71. [2]

Standard 3: Observing, Documenting, and Assessing to Support Young Children and Families

Cohen, D.H., V. Stern, N. Balaban, & N. Gropper. 2008. *Observing and recording the behavior of young children*. 5th ed. New York: Teachers College Press. [3]

DEC (Division for Early Childhood). 2007. Promoting positive outcomes for children with disabilities: Recommendations for curriculum, assessment, and program evaluation. Missoula, MT: Author. www.naeyc.org/about/positions/pdf/PrmtgPositiveOutcomes.pdf [3]

Gonzales-Meña, J. 2005. *Resources for observation and reflection to accompany foundations of early childhood education*. New York: McGraw Hill [3]

Kagan, S.L., C. Scott-Little, & R.M. Clifford. 2003. Assessing young children: What policy makers need to know and do. In *Assessing the state of state assessments: Perspectives on assessing young children*, eds C. Scott-Little, S.L. Kagan, & R.M. Clifford, 25–35. Greensboro, NC: SERVE. [3]

appendix B

Teaching Standards

InTASC Model Core Teaching Standards: A Resource for State Dialogue

Summary of Updated InTASC Core Teaching Standards

The standards have been grouped into four general categories to help users organize their thinking about the standards:

The Learner and Learning

Teaching begins with the learner. To ensure that each student learns new knowledge and skills, teachers must understand that learning and developmental patterns vary among individuals, that learners bring unique individual differences to the learning process, and that learners need supportive and safe learning environments to thrive. Effective teachers have high expectations for each and every learner and implement developmentally appropriate, challenging learning experiences within a variety of learning environments that help all learners meet high standards and reach their full potential. Teachers do this by combining a base of professional knowledge, including an understanding of how cognitive, linguistic, social, emotional, and physical development occurs, with the recognition that learners are individuals who bring differing personal and family backgrounds, skills, abilities, perspectives, talents and interests. Teachers collaborate with learners, colleagues, school leaders, families, members of the learners' communities, and community organizations to better understand their students and maximize their learning. Teachers promote learners' acceptance of responsibility for their own learning and collaborate with them to ensure the effective design and implementation of both self-directed and collaborative learning.

> Standard #1: Learner Development. The teacher understands how learners grow and develop, recognizing that patterns of learning and development vary individually within and across the cognitive, linguistic, social, emotional, and physical areas, and designs and implements developmentally appropriate and challenging learning experiences.

> Standard #2: Learning Differences. The teacher uses understanding of individual differences and diverse cultures and communities to ensure inclusive learning environments that enable each learner to meet high standards.

> Standard #3: Learning Environments. The teacher works with others to create environments that support individual and collaborative learning, and that encourage positive social interaction, active engagement in learning, and self-motivation.

Content

Teachers must have a deep and flexible understanding of their content areas and be able to draw upon content knowledge as they work with learners to access information, apply knowledge in real-world settings, and address meaningful issues to assure learner mastery of the content. Today's teachers make content knowledge accessible to learners by using multiple means of communication, including digital media and information technology. They integrate cross-disciplinary skills (e.g., critical thinking, problem solving, creativity, communication) to help learners use content to propose solutions, forge new understandings, solve problems, and imagine possibilities. Finally, teachers make content knowledge relevant to learners by connecting it to local, state, national, and global issues.

> Standard #4: Content Knowledge. The teacher understands the central concepts, tools of inquiry, and structures of the discipline(s) he or she teaches and creates learning experiences that make the discipline accessible and meaningful for learners to assure mastery of the content.

> Standard #5: Application of Content. The teacher understands how to connect concepts and use differing perspectives to engage learners in critical thinking, creativity, and collaborative problem solving related to authentic local and global issues.

Instructional Practice

Effective instructional practice requires that teachers understand and integrate assessment, planning, and instructional strategies in coordinated and engaging ways. Beginning with their end or goal, teachers first identify student learning objectives and content standards and align assessments to those objectives. Teachers understand how to design, implement and interpret results from a range of formative and summative assessments. This knowledge is integrated into instructional practice so that teachers have access to information that can be used to provide immediate feedback to reinforce student learning and to modify instruction. Planning focuses on using a variety of appropriate and targeted instructional strategies to address diverse ways of learning, to incorporate new technologies to maximize and individualize learning, and to allow learners to take charge of their own learning and do it in creative ways.

Standard #6: Assessment. The teacher understands and uses multiple methods of assessment to engage learners in their own growth, to monitor learner progress, and to guide the teacher's and learner's decision making.

Standard #7: Planning for Instruction. The teacher plans instruction that supports every student in meeting rigorous learning goals by drawing upon knowledge of content areas, curriculum, cross-disciplinary skills, and pedagogy, as well as knowledge of learners and the community context.

Standard #8: Instructional Strategies. The teacher understands and uses a variety of instructional strategies to encourage learners to develop deep understanding of content areas and their connections, and to build skills to apply knowledge in meaningful ways.

Professional Responsibility

Creating and supporting safe, productive learning environments that result in learners achieving at the highest levels is a teacher's primary responsibility. To do this well, teachers must engage in meaningful and intensive professional learning and self-renewal by regularly examining practice through ongoing study, self-reflection, and collaboration. A cycle of continuous self-improvement is enhanced by leadership, collegial support, and collaboration. Active engagement in professional learning and collaboration results in the discovery and implementation of better practice for the purpose of improved teaching and learning. Teachers also contribute to improving instructional practices that meet learners' needs and accomplish their school's mission and goals. Teachers benefit from and participate in collaboration with learners, families, colleagues, other school professionals, and community members. Teachers demonstrate leadership by modeling ethical behavior, contributing to positive changes in practice, and advancing their profession.

Standard #9: Professional Learning and Ethical Practice. The teacher engages in ongoing professional learning and uses evidence to continually evaluate his/her practice, particularly the effects of his/her choices and actions on others (learners, families, other professionals, and the community), and adapts practice to meet the needs of each learner.

Standard #10: Leadership and Collaboration. The teacher seeks appropriate leadership roles and opportunities to take responsibility for student learning, to collaborate with learners, families, colleagues, other school professionals, and community members to ensure learner growth, and to advance the profession.

Standard #1: Learner Development

The teacher understands how learners grow and develop, recognizing that patterns of learning and development vary individually within and across the cognitive, linguistic, social, emotional, and physical areas, and designs and implements developmentally appropriate and challenging learning experiences.

PERFORMANCES

1(a) The teacher regularly assesses individual and group performance in order to design and modify instruction to meet learners' needs in each area of development (cognitive, linguistic, social, emotional, and physical) and scaffolds the next level of development.

1(b) The teacher creates developmentally appropriate instruction that takes into account individual learners' strengths, interests, and needs and that enables each learner to advance and accelerate his/her learning.

1(c) The teacher collaborates with families, communities, colleagues, and other professionals to promote learner growth and development.

ESSENTIAL KNOWLEDGE

1(d) The teacher understands how learning occurs—how learners construct knowledge, acquire skills, and develop disciplined thinking processes—and knows how to use instructional strategies that promote student learning.

1(e) The teacher understands that each learner's cognitive, linguistic, social, emotional, and physical development influences learning and knows how to make instructional decisions that build on learners' strengths and needs.

1(f) The teacher identifies readiness for learning, and understands how development in any one area may affect performance in others.

1(g) The teacher understands the role of language and culture in learning and knows how to modify instruction to make language comprehensible and instruction relevant, accessible, and challenging.

CRITICAL DISPOSITIONS

1(h) The teacher respects learners' differing strengths and needs and is committed to using this information to further each learner's development.

1(i) The teacher is committed to using learners' strengths as a basis for growth, and their misconceptions as opportunities for learning.

1(j) The teacher takes responsibility for promoting learners' growth and development.

1(k) The teacher values the input and contributions of families, colleagues, and other professionals in understanding and supporting each learner's development.

Standard #2: Learning Differences

The teacher uses understanding of individual differences and diverse cultures and communities to ensure inclusive learning environments that enable each learner to meet high standards.

PERFORMANCES

2(a) The teacher designs, adapts, and delivers instruction to address each student's diverse learning strengths and needs and creates opportunities for students to demonstrate their learning in different ways.

2(b) The teacher makes appropriate and timely provisions (e.g., pacing for individual rates of growth, task demands, communication, assessment, and response modes) for individual students with particular learning differences or needs.

2(c) The teacher designs instruction to build on learners' prior knowledge and experiences, allowing learners to accelerate as they demonstrate their understandings.

2(d) The teacher brings multiple perspectives to the discussion of content, including attention to learners' personal, family, and community experiences and cultural norms.

2(e) The teacher incorporates tools of language development into planning and instruction, including strategies for making content accessible to English language learners and for evaluating and supporting their development of English proficiency.

2(f) The teacher accesses resources, supports, and specialized assistance and services to meet particular learning differences or needs.

ESSENTIAL KNOWLEDGE

2(g) The teacher understands and identifies differences in approaches to learning and performance and knows how to design instruction that uses each learner's strengths to promote growth.

2(h) The teacher understands students with exceptional needs, including those associated with disabilities and giftedness, and knows how to use strategies and resources to address these needs.

2(i) The teacher knows about second language acquisition processes and knows how to incorporate instructional strategies and resources to support language acquisition.

2(j) The teacher understands that learners bring assets for learning based on their individual experiences, abilities, talents, prior learning, and peer and social group interactions, as well as language, culture, family, and community values.

2(k) The teacher knows how to access information about the values of diverse cultures and communities and how to incorporate learners' experiences, cultures, and community resources into instruction.

CRITICAL DISPOSITIONS

2(l) The teacher believes that all learners can achieve at high levels and persists in helping each learner reach his/her full potential.

2(m) The teacher respects learners as individuals with differing personal and family backgrounds and various skills, abilities, perspectives, talents, and interests.

2(n) The teacher makes learners feel valued and helps them learn to value each other.

2(o) The teacher values diverse languages and dialects and seeks to integrate them into his/her instructional practice to engage students in learning.

Standard #3: Learning Environments

The teacher works with others to create environments that support individual and collaborative learning, and that encourage positive social interaction, active engagement in learning, and self-motivation.

PERFORMANCES

3(a) The teacher collaborates with learners, families, and colleagues to build a safe, positive learning climate of openness, mutual respect, support, and inquiry.

3(b) The teacher develops learning experiences that engage learners in collaborative and self-directed learning and that extend learner interaction with ideas and people locally and globally.

3(c) The teacher collaborates with learners and colleagues to develop shared values and expectations for respectful interactions, rigorous academic discussions, and individual and group responsibility for quality work.

3(d) The teacher manages the learning environment to actively and equitably engage learners by organizing, allocating, and coordinating the resources of time, space, and learners' attention.

3(e) The teacher uses a variety of methods to engage learners in evaluating the learning environment and collaborates with learners to make appropriate adjustments.

3(f) The teacher communicates verbally and nonverbally in ways that demonstrate respect for and responsiveness to the cultural backgrounds and differing perspectives learners bring to the learning environment.

3(g) The teacher promotes responsible learner use of interactive technologies to extend the possibilities for learning locally and globally.

3(h) The teacher intentionally builds learner capacity to collaborate in face-to-face and virtual environments through applying effective interpersonal communication skills.

ESSENTIAL KNOWLEDGE

3(i) The teacher understands the relationship between motivation and engagement and knows how to design learning experiences using strategies that build learner self-direction and ownership of learning.

3(j) The teacher knows how to help learners work productively and cooperatively with each other to achieve learning goals.

3(k) The teacher knows how to collaborate with learners to establish and monitor elements of a safe and productive learning environment including norms, expectations, routines, and organizational structures.

3(l) The teacher understands how learner diversity can affect communication and knows how to communicate effectively in differing environments.

3(m) The teacher knows how to use technologies and how to guide learners to apply them in appropriate, safe, and effective ways.

CRITICAL DISPOSITIONS

3(n) The teacher is committed to working with learners, colleagues, families, and communities to establish positive and supportive learning environments.

3(o) The teacher values the role of learners in promoting each other's learning and recognizes the importance of peer relationships in establishing a climate of learning.

3(p) The teacher is committed to supporting learners as they participate in decision making, engage in exploration and invention, work collaboratively and independently, and engage in purposeful learning.

3(q) The teacher seeks to foster respectful communication among all members of the learning community.

3(r) The teacher is a thoughtful and responsive listener and observer.

Standard #4: Content Knowledge

The teacher understands the central concepts, tools of inquiry, and structures of the discipline(s) he or she teaches and creates learning experiences that make these aspects of the discipline accessible and meaningful for learners to assure mastery of the content.

PERFORMANCES

4(a) The teacher effectively uses multiple representations and explanations that capture key ideas in the discipline, guide learners through learning progressions, and promote each learner's achievement of content standards.

4(b) The teacher engages students in learning experiences in the discipline(s) that encourage learners to understand, question, and analyze ideas from diverse perspectives so that they master the content.

4(c) The teacher engages learners in applying methods of inquiry and standards of evidence used in the discipline.

4(d) The teacher stimulates learner reflection on prior content knowledge, links new concepts to familiar concepts, and makes connections to learners' experiences.

4(e) The teacher recognizes learner misconceptions in a discipline that interfere with learning, and creates experiences to build accurate conceptual understanding.

4(f) The teacher evaluates and modifies instructional resources and curriculum materials for their comprehensiveness, accuracy for representing particular concepts in the discipline, and appropriateness for his/her learners.

4(g) The teacher uses supplementary resources and technologies effectively to ensure accessibility and relevance for all learners.

4(h) The teacher creates opportunities for students to learn, practice, and master academic language in their content.

4(i) The teacher accesses school and/or district-based resources to evaluate the learner's content knowledge in their primary language.

ESSENTIAL KNOWLEDGE

4(j) The teacher understands major concepts, assumptions, debates, processes of inquiry, and ways of knowing that are central to the discipline(s) s/he teaches.

4(k) The teacher understands common misconceptions in learning the discipline and how to guide learners to accurate conceptual understanding.

4(l) The teacher knows and uses the academic language of the discipline and knows how to make it accessible to learners.

4(m) The teacher knows how to integrate culturally relevant content to build on learners' background knowledge.

4(n) The teacher has a deep knowledge of student content standards and learning progressions in the discipline(s) s/he teaches.

CRITICAL DISPOSITIONS

4(o) The teacher realizes that content knowledge is not a fixed body of facts but is complex, culturally situated, and ever evolving. S/he keeps abreast of new ideas and understandings in the field.

4(p) The teacher appreciates multiple perspectives within the discipline and facilitates learners' critical analysis of these perspectives.

4(q) The teacher recognizes the potential of bias in his/her representation of the discipline and seeks to appropriately address problems of bias.

4(r) The teacher is committed to work toward each learner's mastery of disciplinary content and skills.

Standard #5: Application of Content

The teacher understands how to connect concepts and use differing perspectives to engage learners in critical thinking, creativity, and collaborative problem solving related to authentic local and global issues.

PERFORMANCES

5(a) The teacher develops and implements projects that guide learners in analyzing the complexities of an issue or question using perspectives from varied disciplines and cross-disciplinary skills (e.g., a water quality study that draws upon biology and chemistry to look at factual information and social studies to examine policy implications).

5(b) The teacher engages learners in applying content knowledge to real-world problems through the lens of interdisciplinary themes (e.g., financial literacy, environmental literacy).

5(c) The teacher facilitates learners' use of current tools and resources to maximize content learning in varied contexts.

5(d) The teacher engages learners in questioning and challenging assumptions and approaches in order to foster innovation and problem solving in local and global contexts.

5(e) The teacher develops learners' communication skills in disciplinary and interdisciplinary contexts by creating meaningful opportunities to employ a variety of forms of communication that address varied audiences and purposes.

5(f) The teacher engages learners in generating and evaluating new ideas and novel approaches, seeking inventive solutions to problems, and developing original work.

5(g) The teacher facilitates learners' ability to develop diverse social and cultural perspectives that expand their understanding of local and global issues and create novel approaches to solving problems.

5(h) The teacher develops and implements supports for learner literacy development across content areas.

ESSENTIAL KNOWLEDGE

5(i) The teacher understands the ways of knowing in his/her discipline, how it relates to other disciplinary approaches to inquiry, and the strengths and limitations of each approach in addressing problems, issues, and concerns.

5(j) The teacher understands how current interdisciplinary themes (e.g., civic literacy, health literacy, global awareness) connect to the core subjects and knows how to weave those themes into meaningful learning experiences.

5(k) The teacher understands the demands of accessing and managing information as well as how to evaluate issues of ethics and quality related to information and its use.

5(l) The teacher understands how to use digital and interactive technologies for efficiently and effectively achieving specific learning goals.

5(m) The teacher understands critical thinking processes and knows how to help learners develop high level questioning skills to promote their independent learning.

5(n) The teacher understands communication modes and skills as vehicles for learning (e.g., information gathering and processing) across disciplines as well as vehicles for expressing learning.

5(o) The teacher understands creative thinking processes and how to engage learners in producing original work.

5(p) The teacher knows where and how to access resources to build global awareness and understanding, and how to integrate them into the curriculum.

CRITICAL DISPOSITIONS

5(q) The teacher is constantly exploring how to use disciplinary knowledge as a lens to address local and global issues.

5(r) The teacher values knowledge outside his/her own content area and how such knowledge enhances student learning.

5(s) The teacher values flexible learning environments that encourage learner exploration, discovery, and expression across content areas.

Standard #6: Assessment

The teacher understands and uses multiple methods of assessment to engage learners in their own growth, to monitor learner progress, and to guide the teacher's and learner's decision making.

PERFORMANCES

6(a) The teacher balances the use of formative and summative assessment as appropriate to support, verify, and document learning.

6(b) The teacher designs assessments that match learning objectives with assessment methods and minimizes sources of bias that can distort assessment results.

6(c) The teacher works independently and collaboratively to examine test and other performance data to understand each learner's progress and to guide planning.

6(d) The teacher engages learners in understanding and identifying quality work and provides them with effective descriptive feedback to guide their progress toward that work.

6(e) The teacher engages learners in multiple ways of demonstrating knowledge and skill as part of the assessment process.

6(f) The teacher models and structures processes that guide learners in examining their own thinking and learning as well as the performance of others.

6(g) The teacher effectively uses multiple and appropriate types of assessment data to identify each student's learning needs and to develop differentiated learning experiences.

6(h) The teacher prepares all learners for the demands of particular assessment formats and makes appropriate accommodations in assessments or testing conditions, especially for learners with disabilities and language learning needs.

6(i) The teacher continually seeks appropriate ways to employ technology to support assessment practice both to engage learners more fully and to assess and address learner needs.

ESSENTIAL KNOWLEDGE

6(j) The teacher understands the differences between formative and summative applications of assessment and knows how and when to use each.

6(k) The teacher understands the range of types and multiple purposes of assessment and how to design, adapt, or select appropriate assessments to address specific learning goals and individual differences, and to minimize sources of bias.

6(l) The teacher knows how to analyze assessment data to understand patterns and gaps in learning, to guide planning and instruction, and to provide meaningful feedback to all learners.

6(m) The teacher knows when and how to engage learners in analyzing their own assessment results and in helping to set goals for their own learning.

6(n) The teacher understands the positive impact of effective descriptive feedback for learners and knows a variety of strategies for communicating this feedback.

6(o) The teacher knows when and how to evaluate and report learner progress against standards.

6(p) The teacher understands how to prepare learners for assessments and how to make accommodations in assessments and testing conditions, especially for learners with disabilities and language learning needs.

CRITICAL DISPOSITIONS

6(q) The teacher is committed to engaging learners actively in assessment processes and to developing each learner's capacity to review and communicate about their own progress and learning.

6(r) The teacher takes responsibility for aligning instruction and assessment with learning goals.

6(s) The teacher is committed to providing timely and effective descriptive feedback to learners on their progress.

6(t) The teacher is committed to using multiple types of assessment processes to support, verify, and document learning.

6(u) The teacher is committed to making accommodations in assessments and testing conditions, especially for learners with disabilities and language learning needs.

6(v) The teacher is committed to the ethical use of various assessments and assessment data to identify learner strengths and needs to promote learner growth.

Standard #7: Planning for Instruction

The teacher plans instruction that supports every student in meeting rigorous learning goals by drawing upon knowledge of content areas, curriculum, cross-disciplinary skills, and pedagogy, as well as knowledge of learners and the community context.

PERFORMANCES

7(a) The teacher individually and collaboratively selects and creates learning experiences that are appropriate for curriculum goals and content standards, and are relevant to learners.

7(b) The teacher plans how to achieve each student's learning goals, choosing appropriate strategies and accommodations, resources, and materials to differentiate instruction for individuals and groups of learners.

7(c) The teacher develops appropriate sequencing of learning experiences and provides multiple ways to demonstrate knowledge and skill.

7(d) The teacher plans for instruction based on formative and summative assessment data, prior learner knowledge, and learner interest.

7(e) The teacher plans collaboratively with professionals who have specialized expertise (e.g., special educators, related service providers, language learning specialists, librarians, media specialists) to design and jointly deliver as appropriate learning experiences to meet unique learning needs.

7(f) The teacher evaluates plans in relation to short- and long-range goals and systematically adjusts plans to meet each student's learning needs and enhance learning.

ESSENTIAL KNOWLEDGE

7(g) The teacher understands content and content standards and how these are organized in the curriculum.

7(h) The teacher understands how integrating cross-disciplinary skills in instruction engages learners purposefully in applying content knowledge.

7(i) The teacher understands learning theory, human development, cultural diversity, and individual differences and how these impact ongoing planning.

7(j) The teacher understands the strengths and needs of individual learners and how to plan instruction that is responsive to these strengths and needs.

7(k) The teacher knows a range of evidence-based instructional strategies, resources, and technological tools and how to use them effectively to plan instruction that meets diverse learning needs.

7(l) The teacher knows when and how to adjust plans based on assessment information and learner responses.

7(m) The teacher knows when and how to access resources and collaborate with others to support student learning (e.g., special educators, related service providers, language learner specialists, librarians, media specialists, community organizations).

CRITICAL DISPOSITIONS

7(n) The teacher respects learners' diverse strengths and needs and is committed to using this information to plan effective instruction.

7(o) The teacher values planning as a collegial activity that takes into consideration the input of learners, colleagues, families, and the larger community.

7(p) The teacher takes professional responsibility to use short- and long-term planning as a means of assuring student learning.

7(q) The teacher believes that plans must always be open to adjustment and revision based on learner needs and changing circumstances.

Standard #8: Instructional Strategies

The teacher understands and uses a variety of instructional strategies to encourage learners to develop deep understanding of content areas and their connections, and to build skills to apply knowledge in meaningful ways.

PERFORMANCES

8(a) The teacher uses appropriate strategies and resources to adapt instruction to the needs of individuals and groups of learners.

8(b) The teacher continuously monitors student learning, engages learners in assessing their progress, and adjusts instruction in response to student learning needs.

8(c) The teacher collaborates with learners to design and implement relevant learning experiences, identify their strengths, and access family and community resources to develop their areas of interest.

8(d) The teacher varies his/her role in the instructional process (e.g., instructor, facilitator, coach, audience) in relation to the content and purposes of instruction and the needs of learners.

8(e) The teacher provides multiple models and representations of concepts and skills with opportunities for learners to demonstrate their knowledge through a variety of products and performances.

8(f) The teacher engages all learners in developing higher order questioning skills and metacognitive processes.

8(g) The teacher engages learners in using a range of learning skills and technology tools to access, interpret, evaluate, and apply information.

8(h) The teacher uses a variety of instructional strategies to support and expand learners' communication through speaking, listening, reading, writing, and other modes.

8(i) The teacher asks questions to stimulate discussion that serves different purposes (e.g., probing for learner understanding, helping learners articulate their ideas and thinking processes, stimulating curiosity, and helping learners to question).

ESSENTIAL KNOWLEDGE

8(j) The teacher understands the cognitive processes associated with various kinds of learning (e.g., critical and creative thinking, problem framing and problem solving, invention, memorization and recall) and how these processes can be stimulated.

8(k) The teacher knows how to apply a range of developmentally, culturally, and linguistically appropriate instructional strategies to achieve learning goals.

8(l) The teacher knows when and how to use appropriate strategies to differentiate instruction and engage all learners in complex thinking and meaningful tasks.

8(m) The teacher understands how multiple forms of communication (oral, written, nonverbal, digital, visual) convey ideas, foster self-expression, and build relationships.

8(n) The teacher knows how to use a wide variety of resources, including human and technological, to engage students in learning.

8(o) The teacher understands how content and skill development can be supported by media and technology and knows how to evaluate these resources for quality, accuracy, and effectiveness.

CRITICAL DISPOSITIONS

8(p) The teacher is committed to deepening awareness and understanding the strengths and needs of diverse learners when planning and adjusting instruction.

8(q) The teacher values the variety of ways people communicate and encourages learners to develop and use multiple forms of communication.

8(r) The teacher is committed to exploring how the use of new and emerging technologies can support and promote student learning.

8(s) The teacher values flexibility and reciprocity in the teaching process as necessary for adapting instruction to learner responses, ideas, and needs.

Standard #9: Professional Learning and Ethical Practice

The teacher engages in ongoing professional learning and uses evidence to continually evaluate his/her practice, particularly the effects of his/her choices and actions on others (learners, families, other professionals, and the community), and adapts practice to meet the needs of each learner.

PERFORMANCES

9(a) The teacher engages in ongoing learning opportunities to develop knowledge and skills in order to provide all learners with engaging curriculum and learning experiences based on local and state standards.

9(b) The teacher engages in meaningful and appropriate professional learning experiences aligned with his/her own needs and the needs of the learners, school, and system.

9(c) Independently and in collaboration with colleagues, the teacher uses a variety of data (e.g., systematic observation, information about learners, research) to evaluate the outcomes of teaching and learning and to adapt planning and practice.

9(d) The teacher actively seeks professional, community, and technological resources, within and outside the school, as supports for analysis, reflection, and problem-solving.

9(e) The teacher reflects on his/her personal biases and accesses resources to deepen his/her own understanding of cultural, ethnic, gender, and learning differences to build stronger relationships and create more relevant learning experiences.

9(f) The teacher advocates, models, and teaches safe, legal, and ethical use of information and technology including appropriate documentation of sources and respect for others in the use of social media.

ESSENTIAL KNOWLEDGE

9(g) The teacher understands and knows how to use a variety of self-assessment and problem-solving strategies to analyze and reflect on his/her practice and to plan for adaptations/adjustments.

9(h) The teacher knows how to use learner data to analyze practice and differentiate instruction accordingly.

9(i) The teacher understands how personal identity, worldview, and prior experience affect perceptions and expectations, and recognizes how they may bias behaviors and interactions with others.

9(j) The teacher understands laws related to learners' rights and teacher responsibilities (e.g., for educational equity, appropriate education for learners with disabilities, confidentiality, privacy, appropriate treatment of learners, reporting in situations related to possible child abuse).

9(k) The teacher knows how to build and implement a plan for professional growth directly aligned with his/her needs as a growing professional using feedback from teacher evaluations and observations, data on learner performance, and school- and system-wide priorities.

CRITICAL DISPOSITIONS

9(l) The teacher takes responsibility for student learning and uses ongoing analysis and reflection to improve planning and practice.

9(m) The teacher is committed to deepening understanding of his/her own frames of reference (e.g., culture, gender, language, abilities, ways of knowing), the potential biases in these frames, and their impact on expectations for and relationships with learners and their families.

9(n) The teacher sees him/herself as a learner, continuously seeking opportunities to draw upon current education policy and research as sources of analysis and reflection to improve practice.

9(o) The teacher understands the expectations of the profession including codes of ethics, professional standards of practice, and relevant law and policy.

Standard #10: Leadership and Collaboration

The teacher seeks appropriate leadership roles and opportunities to take responsibility for student learning, to collaborate with learners, families, colleagues, other school professionals, and community members to ensure learner growth, and to advance the profession.

PERFORMANCES

10(a) The teacher takes an active role on the instructional team, giving and receiving feedback on practice, examining learner work, analyzing data from multiple sources, and sharing responsibility for decision making and accountability for each student's learning.

10(b) The teacher works with other school professionals to plan and jointly facilitate learning on how to meet diverse needs of learners.

10(c) The teacher engages collaboratively in the school-wide effort to build a shared vision and supportive culture, identify common goals, and monitor and evaluate progress toward those goals.

10(d) The teacher works collaboratively with learners and their families to establish mutual expectations and ongoing communication to support learner development and achievement.

10(e) Working with school colleagues, the teacher builds ongoing connections with community resources to enhance student learning and well being.

10(f) The teacher engages in professional learning, contributes to the knowledge and skill of others, and works collaboratively to advance professional practice.

10(g) The teacher uses technological tools and a variety of communication strategies to build local and global learning communities that engage learners, families, and colleagues.

10(h) The teacher uses and generates meaningful research on education issues and policies.

10(i) The teacher seeks appropriate opportunities to model effective practice for colleagues, to lead professional learning activities, and to serve in other leadership roles.

10(j) The teacher advocates to meet the needs of learners, to strengthen the learning environment, and to enact system change.

10(k) The teacher takes on leadership roles at the school, district, state, and/or national level and advocates for learners, the school, the community, and the profession.

ESSENTIAL KNOWLEDGE

10(l) The teacher understands schools as organizations within a historical, cultural, political, and social context and knows how to work with others across the system to support learners.

10(m) The teacher understands that alignment of family, school, and community spheres of influence enhances student learning and that discontinuity in these spheres of influence interferes with learning.

10(n) The teacher knows how to work with other adults and has developed skills in collaborative interaction appropriate for both face-to-face and virtual contexts.

10(o) The teacher knows how to contribute to a common culture that supports high expectations for student learning.

CRITICAL DISPOSITIONS

10(p) The teacher actively shares responsibility for shaping and supporting the mission of his/her school as one of advocacy for learners and accountability for their success.

10(q) The teacher respects families' beliefs, norms, and expectations and seeks to work collaboratively with learners and families in setting and meeting challenging goals.

10(r) The teacher takes initiative to grow and develop with colleagues through interactions that enhance practice and support student learning.

10(s) The teacher takes responsibility for contributing to and advancing the profession.

10(t) The teacher embraces the challenge of continuous improvement and change.

Reference Chart of Key Cross-Cutting Themes in Updated InTASC Standards

This chart shows where in the text of the standards certain key themes are referenced, demonstrating how they have been integrated across the document. In some instances, the key theme is not explicit but can be inferred.

Theme	Knowledge	Disposition	Performance
*Collaboration	3(j), 3(k), 3(i), 5(p), 7(m), 10(l), 10(n)	1(k), 3(n), 3(o), 3(p), 6(q), 6(s), 7(o), 9(l), 10(q), 10(r)	1(c), 3(a), 3(b), 3(c), 3(e), 3(h), 6(c), 7(a), 7(e), 8(b), 8(c), 9(a–d), 10(a–g)
*Communication	3(l), 3(j), 5(n), 6(l), 6(n), 6(o), 8(m), 10(n)	3(q), 3(r), 6(q), 6(s), 8(q)	3(c), 3(e), 3(f), 3(h), 5(e), 6(d), 6(e), 8(h), 8(i), 10(g)
*Creativity/Innovation	5(l), 5(o), 8(j), 8(m)	3(p), 5(s)	5(d), 5(f), 5(g), 8(i), 9(f)
*Critical thinking, problem solving	4(j), 4(k), 4(l), 5(i), 5(m), 8(j), 8(l), 9(g)	4(p), 4(r), 5(q)	4(b), 4(c), 4(d), 4(e), 4(h), 5(a), 5(b), 5(d), 5(f), 5(g), 6(f), 8(f), 8(g), 8(i), 9(d)
Cultural competence	1(g), 2(g), 2(j), 2(k), 3(i), 4(k), 4(m), 7(i), 8(k), 9(i)	4(o), 8(t), 9(m)	2(d), 3(f), 5(h), 7(c), 9(e)
English language learners	1(g), 2(i), 2(j), 6(p), 7(m), 8(m)	2(o), 6(u)	2(d), 2(e), 4(i), 6(h), 7(e)
Families/Communities	2(j), 2(k), 10(m)	1(k), 2(m), 3(n), 7(o), 9(m), 10(q)	1(c), 2(d), 3(a), 8(c), 9(b), 10(c), 10(d), 10(e), 10(g), 10(k)
Individual differences	1(d-g), 2(g), 2(h), 2(j), 2(k), 3(l), 4(l), 4(m), 6(k), 6(l), 6(m), 6(o), 6(p), 7(i–m), 8(k), 8(l), 9(g), 9(h), 9(i), 9(j)	1(h), 1(i), 1(k), 2(l), 2(m), 2(n), 2(o), 4(r), 6(q), 6(s), 6(u), 7(n), 7(q), 8(p), 8(s), 9(m)	1(a), 1(b), 2(a–f), 2(h), 3(d), 3(f), 4(a), 4(d), 4(e), 4(f), 4(g), 6(c), 6(d), 6(g), 6(h), 6(i), 7(b), 7(c), 7(d–f),8(a), 8(b), 8(d), 8(e), 8(f), 9(a), 9(c), 9(e),10(a). 10(b)
Interdisciplinary themes	5(j)	5(q–s)	5(c), 5(b), 5(e)
Leadership	1(c), 3(k), 5(p), 7(l), 7(m), 8(l), 8(n), 9(i), 9(j), 10(l–o)	1(j), 3(n), 4(p), 5(q), 6(r), 6(v), 7(o), 7(p), 8(s), 9(m), 9(n), 10(p–t)	2(f), 3(a), 3(c), 3(d), 4(g), 5(d), 5(g), 6(c), 6(e), 6(f), 7(a), 7(e), 8(c), 8(d), 9(a–f), 10(a–k)
*Multiple perspectives	5(i), 5(j), 5(n), 5(p), 9(i), 7(h), 10(l), 10(m)	4(p), 5(r), 6(t)	2(d), 3(e), 4(b), 5(a), 5(b), 5(d), 5(e), 5(g)
Professional learning	6(j–p), 7(f), 7(k), 8(k), 8(n), 8(o), 9(g–k)	4(o), 4(p), 4(q), 5(q), 5(r), 6(t), 8(p), 9(l–o), 10(r), 10(s), 10(t)	6(a), 6(c), 6(g), 6(i), 8(g), 9(a–f), 10(f), 10(h)
Student-directed learning	3(i), 3(k), 5(m), 6(m)	3(n), 3(o), 3(p), 6(q), 6(s), 10(q)	3(b), 3(c), 5(d), 5(f), 6(f), 8(b), 8(c)
Teacher responsibility	3(m), 5(l), 9(j), 9(k), 10(o)	1(j), 4(o), 4(q), 5(r), 6(r), 6(t), 6(u), 6(v), 7(p), 9(l–o), 10(p), 10(r), 10(s)	3(c), 3(g), 5(h), 9(e), 9(f)
*Technology	3(j), 3(m), 5(k), 5(l), 7(k), 8(n), 8(o), 10(n)	8(q), 8(r)	3(g), 3(h), 4(g), 5(c), 6(i), 8(g), 9(d), 9(f),10(e), 10(g)
Use of data to support learning	5(k), 6(j–p), 7(l), 8(n), 8(o), 9(g), 9(h), 9(k)	6(q–v), 7(q), 8(s), 9(l)	2(d), 5(c), 5(f), 6(a–i), 8(b), 8(d), 8(g), 9(c), 9(f), 10(a–c)

*Cross-disciplinary skills